Foreign Languages in the primary school

Modern Foreign Languages
in the primary school

the
what, why & how
of early MFL teaching

Keith Sharpe

KOGAN
PAGE

First published in 2001

Kogan Page Limited
120 Pentonville Road
London N1 9JN
UK

Stylus Publishing Inc.
22883 Quicksilver Drive
Sterling VA 20166-2012
USA

British Library Cataloguing in Publication Data

A CIP record for this book is available from the British Library.

ISBN 0 7494 3609 3

Typeset by Jean Cussons Typesetting, Diss, Norfolk
Printed and bound in Great Britain by Biddles Ltd, Guildford and King's Lynn

Contents

Preface

The teaching of modern foreign languages in the primary school is now high on the agenda in England, and it is rapidly becoming common practice in countries across the world. This book offers an explanation of this phenomenon and puts forward ideas as to how primary modern foreign languages can be taught and why they should be taught to all young children. It is addressed to primary and secondary teachers, headteachers, student trainee teachers, governors, LEA officers, educational consultants, parents and anyone interested in promoting the early learning of modern languages. It is based on the author's experience as a teacher, teacher trainer and researcher.

This book seeks a balance between being overly academic on the one hand and too much of a 'tips for teachers' manual on the other. It makes some references to research and published scholarly literature, but tries to avoid being excessively scholastic. It makes some reference to practical classroom activities, but it does not purport to be a teacher's handbook, teaching syllabus or curriculum resource. Its objectives will have been met if it provokes some thought and reflection about the future place of modern foreign languages in primary schooling.

It advocates the case for empowering primary generalist teachers to take responsibility for delivering a modern language curriculum to primary pupils. It does this because we need to avoid making the mistakes that were made with primary schooling in England when the National Curriculum as a whole was first introduced in 1988. Repeated versions of programmes of study, often written by groups on which primary specialists were not well represented, failed properly to take account of the realities of the primary classroom. Time and public money were wasted. Primary teachers and headteachers were put under unnecessarily high levels of stress. Pupils' learning across the curriculum was rendered less effective than it might have been. We need to learn from this hard experience in planning now for the teaching of foreign languages in the primary school. We need to get it right.

Among those with an interest in the subject there is some difference of view as to what it should be called. In Scotland the phrase 'modern languages in the primary school' is generally preferred, and this is usually abbreviated to MLPS. South of the border the term 'primary modern foreign languages' is more common. This equally cumbersome phrase is generally shortened to primary MFL, and this phrase is used throughout this book.

The instances of primary MFL teaching given in this book all use French as linguistic examples. It would have been possible to give multilingual examples, or to have used only English. English alone seemed inadequate to give a proper 'flavour' of MFL teaching. And given that the book is aimed mainly at an English audience who are more likely to have encountered this foreign language than any other, it seemed sensible to make French the case study for illustrative purposes so as to retain the 'foreign' element in MFL but maximize the likelihood of easy comprehension. It should though be borne in mind that the arguments advanced in the book are intended to apply to modern foreign languages generally.

The book is organized in five parts based on five fundamental issues:

- *Why* primary MFL should be taught.
- *What* and *when* primary MFL should be taught.
- *Who* should teach primary MFL.
- *How* primary MFL should be taught.
- *Future developments* in primary MFL.

This book has been written in the first year of the new millennium, a time of excitement and hope for the future. The Year 2000 National Curriculum, which took effect from September 2000, makes specific reference to primary MFL teaching for the first time. In this atmosphere of hope and expectation the book seeks to make a contribution to the debate now emerging as to how the subject can be implemented successfully.

Part 1

The 'why' issues

1
More phoenix than dodo now

Lack of primary MFL teaching in England

Delivering the annual Romanes lecture at the Sheldonian Theatre, Oxford, in December 1999, Tony Blair (who became UK prime minister in 1997) emphasized the importance of children learning a modern language at a young age:

> English may be the new lingua franca, a competitive advantage for us as a nation, not least in education. But the competitive advantage for each of us as individuals is the capacity to make our way as freely as possible through the new Europe and the wider world. Everyone knows that with languages the earlier you start, the easier they are. The National Curriculum rightly makes a modern language compulsory from the beginning of secondary school. But many children gain a valuable head start earlier. Some primary schools already do excellent work in this area, and language teaching from the age of seven or eight is almost universal in independent schools, once competence in the basics has been achieved. As all schools move towards universal competence in literacy and numeracy, the scope for more language teaching in the later primary years is something we are seriously considering.

It is quite a sobering thought that the 19th and 20th centuries passed almost entirely without anything firm about the teaching of modern foreign languages in English primary schools being said by any British prime minister or secretary of state for education. Then in the final month of the second millennium, at the eleventh hour so to speak, the British government announces that it is 'seriously considering' the issue. Virtually alone amongst developed countries in general, and the European nations in particular, the English education system which was built up over centuries has never formally required its primary-age children to learn a foreign language. Furthermore, the fact that Mr Blair's government declared itself to be 'seriously considering' primary MFL is not per se necessarily cause for great optimism. Earlier in the 20th century a previous government spoke in similar terms, but eventually it all came to nought.

Although modern languages, particularly French, had long been thought a suitable subject for inclusion in the curricula of independent fee charging 'preparatory' schools, it was not until the 1960s that the possibility of offering a modern language in state primary schools was contemplated in government circles. In 1963 the then minister of education, Sir Edward Boyle, gave government support to a 'pilot scheme to test the feasibility of starting French from the age of eight' which was to receive funding from the Nuffield Foundation to the tune of £100,000 (approximately £2 million now). This was a period of relative prosperity after the austerity of the immediate post-war period. The then prime minister, Harold Macmillan, had just told the nation that people had 'never had it so good'. It was also a period in which Britain was finding a new post-imperial role in the world. The Federation of British Industry supported the initiative, and there was enthusiasm and interest from many quarters. However, even at this early stage concerns were raised which dogged the project throughout, some of which still have currency in contemporary debates about the place of modern foreign languages in primary education. These included the following:

- Which language should be taught?
- How can sufficient appropriately trained and qualified teachers be found?
- What teaching methods are effective in teaching foreign languages?
- Should the government determine what is to be taught?

The pilot scheme lasted barely a decade and was effectively brought to an abrupt end by the unambiguous and fateful conclusion of the evaluation report produced by the National Foundation for Educational Research (NFER) in 1974 which declared that:

> ... it is difficult to resist the conclusion that the weight of evidence has combined with the balance of opinion to tip the scales against a possible expansion of the teaching of French in primary schools. (Burstall *et al*, 1974: 246)

This dismal outcome was apparently justified by the fact that the evaluators found no substantial differences in later achievement at secondary school between those pupils who had been taught French for three years in the primary school and those who had not. The validity of this finding was challenged by many at the time (see for example: Gamble and Smalley, 1975; Buckby, 1976; Gamble and Hoy, 1977), principally on three fairly damaging grounds. Firstly, the sample of pupils studied dwindled over time to very small numbers whose eventual representativeness of all the children who took part in the project was highly questionable. Secondly, the validity and reliability of some of the test procedures used were dubious. And finally no account was taken of what the secondary schools did, which in most cases was nothing. They did not generally discriminate between incoming pupils who had done primary French and incoming pupils who had not done primary French. Most commonly they simply treated them all the same, which amounted to subjecting all pupils to a 'start again as if they know nothing' policy. As a statement on foreign languages in the primary curriculum drafted by Bedfordshire LEA, one of the authorities involved from 1964 onwards in the primary French project, pointed out:

> All the early documentation stressed the need for primary/secondary continuity and it was stipulated that pupils entering secondary schools from primary schools in the pilot scheme must be taught separately from beginners in French. Unfortunately this recommendation was never enforced and most children found themselves treated as beginners again at the age of 11. This consideration never formed part of the NFER research into the pilot scheme and the 1974 conclusions about children's achievement took no account of what had happened five years earlier.

This last criticism is particularly damning. The failure to consider the effect of the attitude of secondary schools is a very serious omission. What must it have been like for primary pupils who had studied French for three years to be treated in their first year of secondary schooling as if they knew nothing? Faced with pupils from pilot and non-pilot feeder primary schools, secondary teachers apparently felt they had no option but to 'start from scratch'. It is arguable that under these circumstances it is surprising that the pilot scheme pupils did not do worse than the non-pilot pupils. What came to be known as the Burstall Report really gave no indication of how valuable primary French, or any other foreign language, could be where proper provision for progression and continuity into the secondary phase was made. Despite this it was taken as grounds for ending any further government support for primary MFL, and this continued to be the position throughout the rest of the 20th century. Except in areas where there was a particular commitment on the part of the LEA, and in a few schools where there were individual enthusiasts, primary MFL in England and elsewhere in the UK died out.

There are many lessons to learn from the fate of this pilot project in post-war England, but the stark reality remains that after this brief experiment with primary MFL, which actually affected the lives of only a small minority of pupils, the broad status quo was re-established where children are taught

French and other languages in private schools but not in the primary schools attended by the mass of the population.

Why should it be that the independent sector takes it as a sine qua non that primary MFL teaching is a good thing, while those responsible for the state system have continued not to do so? This is after all the only curriculum area in which such a discrepancy exists. There is otherwise a fairly clear consensus on what subjects should be included in the primary curriculum for children of junior age. To some extent at least an answer is to be found in the perceived aims and objective espoused by the two sectors. As Alexander (1984) has pointed out, the primary school system inherited many of the traditions and much of the culture of the elementary schools which emerged after the 1870 Education Act. Broadly speaking, the underling philosophy of elementary schooling can be characterized as essentially utilitarian: pupils were to be taught what it was considered useful for them to know and to be able to do. The traditions of the independent preparatory schools were, and to a considerable extent continue to be, associated with the 'public schools', and through them with the culture of the older established universities. This culture can be characterized as essentially idealistic: these institutions embodied certain ideals which were set before pupils as models towards which they were expected to aspire. Within the ideal conception of 'an educated person' knowledge of classical and modern languages played an important role because of the access they gave to works of great literature which were seen as central to the cultivation of the mind and initiation into Culture with a capital C. Over time, of course, the distinction between the two cultures of schooling has become less marked, with modern primary schools concerned to deliver a much broader curriculum than the old elementary diet of reading, 'riting and 'rithmetic, and independent schools adopting a more instrumental approach to marketing themselves in terms of promoting pupils' success in public examinations. Nevertheless it is arguably in the case of foreign language teaching that the major continuing distinction is most clear, perhaps because the usefulness of the subject has never been fully recognized in England; it may be an accomplishment of the educated person but is not yet seen as a positive asset, still less a necessity, as is the case in other countries outside the English-speaking world. The pre-eminence of English as a world language has tended to reinforce the idea that it is not really necessary or useful for native speakers of English to learn to speak another language. The implicit assumption is that since you can count on the natives to speak English there is no pressing need to speak the language of the natives. A few years ago a joke doing the rounds of teachers of modern languages parodied this attitude.

Question: What do you call a person who can speak three languages? Answer: Trilingual.

Question: What do you call a person who can speak two languages?
Answer: Bilingual.
Question: What do you call a person who can speak only one language?
Answer: English.

In the case of English English, as against other kinds of English such as American English, this a priori invitation to linguistic idleness is strongly rein-forced by Britain's imperial history, and an even deeper attitudinal legacy passing down the ages from generation to generation which might be summarized as an 'island mentality'. In his insightful study of the English, Paxman (1999) traces the origins of such insularity through the centuries, quoting, for example, Shakespeare, who in the words of John of Gaunt in *Richard II* speaks of:

This fortress built by Nature for herself
Against infection and the hand of war,
This happy breed of men, this little world;
This precious stone set in the silver sea,
Which serves it in the office of a wall,
Or as a moat defensive to a house.

and George Orwell who noted that:

During the war of 1914–18 the English working class were in contact with foreigners to an extent that is rarely possible. The sole result was that they brought back a hatred of all Europeans, except the Germans, whose courage they admired. In four years on French soil they did not even acquire a liking for wine. (Quoted in Paxman, 1999: 29)

It is largely this heritage which underpins the apocryphal tales of the English abroad whose attempts to communicate consist mainly of speaking their own language more loudly. It is of course an open question as to whether increasing foreign travel in the latter half of the 20th century really wrought any fundamental change in English attitudes.

The perceived 'failure' of the one major national trial in teaching a modern language at the primary stage is itself testimony to the official English view that the only real criterion is 'usefulness'. The overwhelming emphasis of the NFER evaluation of the Primary French Project reported by Burstall *et al* (1974) is put on the issue of whether or not teaching French from the age of eight produces measurably better results in examinations taken at the end of secondary schooling. This is an unequivocally utilitarian approach: it is the concern with specific assessible short-term pay-offs at a subsequent stage in schooling rather than an interest in the intrinsic value of the experience itself for young children. It also ignores wider and more diffuse benefits, or those which occur later in life. However, in this regard all educators and policy-makers of a utilitarian frame of mind might do well to bear in mind the warning of a schoolmaster writing in the Centenary Magazine of the Liverpool Institute High School for Boys in 1925:

> In estimating the worth of any school it is futile to enumerate the successes of one year or of one period by counting up the open scholarships... What is needed is some estimate of the effect on each boy turned out year by year... Only old pupils, looking back on their school-life and seeing the effect on their own minds and characters, and multiplying that effect by thousands, can arrive somewhere near the truth. (Quoted in Hawkins, 1999: 36)

To the view that the worthiness of primary MFL should be judged only in terms of how useful they are can be added the difficulties inherent in actually providing them. It is the case that there just have not been the teachers that would be required to deliver the subject in all primary schools, neither specialist teachers of MFL who could go into primary schools on a peri-patetic basis to teach a series of classes, nor the generalist primary practitioners who might include MFL amongst the areas they can offer to include in the curriculum they teach to their own classes. To a large extent this state of affairs has operated as a self-reproducing cycle. Because foreign language learning is not much valued in England generally, levels of linguistic competence are relatively low and specialist teachers of MFL relatively few in number. Before the introduction of the National Curriculum many children dropped MFL as a subject during the years of secondary schooling and large numbers of pupils were not taught the subject at all. Ever since the introduction of the National Curriculum following the Education Reform Act of 1988 (discussed in some detail in the Chapter 2), which of course only provided a MFL entitlement for pupils of secondary school age, there have been chronic shortages of MFL teachers. These have persisted despite reductions in the extent of the original scope of pupils' MFL entitlement. The same self-reinforcing cycle operates at the level of the primary generalists. Whereas most entrants to primary initial teacher training will have some background from their own secondary schooling of the subjects taught in the primary curriculum, only a small number arrive with a strength in MFL, and although it is possible that they could build on whatever limited base they have during the period of training, there has until recently been what might be termed a 'silent conspiracy' between the policy makers who have no desire to resource additional support for MFL and teacher training students who have no desire to learn to teach the subject. Given the enormous pressures the National Curriculum has put on primary teachers since 1988, it is understandable that both parties should think they have enough to do without taking on the headache of yet another subject, and particularly one which is not popular nor much culturally valued.

Thus it was that from 1975 onwards the idea of teaching modern languages in the primary school in England became been pretty much a 'dead duck'. In most places it became extinct, and like the dodo, had been heard of but was to be seen no more. Unlike the dodo, however, its extinction was not complete and it was not permanent. Indeed it was possible to argue at the beginning of the final decade of the 20th century that the teaching of primary MFL was 'more phoenix than dodo now' (Sharpe, 1991).

The resurrection of primary MFL teaching

An educational phoenix is a rare phenomenon. Most innovations which have their day and then die stay dead. The Initial Teaching Alphabet and programmed learning, for example, both blossomed and flourished for a while, then withered and died without hope of resurrection. After the kiss of death administered to primary French by Clare Burstall's devastating NFER report, rigor mortis gradually set in. Central government funding dried up, and with a few noble, laudable and honourable exceptions local government funding followed suit. With the means of survival withdrawn, primary teaching of modern languages was consigned to the ashes. It was, however, not to remain there. Like the famous bird of mythology which rose from the ashes to fly again, primary MFL, especially primary French, began to make a comeback in the late 1980s and early 1990s. At that stage there were beginning to appear some signs of life, giving grounds, if not for sure and certain hope, at least for believing resurrection to be a possibility.

Amongst the first signs of hope was the interim report of the National Curriculum Modern Languages Working Group (NCMLWG), set up alongside other working groups to design what would become the first national statutorily required formal curriculum. Alone amongst the National Curriculum working groups, this group's members had to deal with a subject which only covered the years 11–16 rather than 5–16 like all the rest. And yet they had to fit in with the same 10-level assessment framework designed to cover 11 years of compulsory schooling which the national Task Group on Assessment and Testing (TGAT) had proposed for all subjects. What were they to do? They could have made MFL an exception and used less than 10 levels to reflect the fact that their curriculum prescriptions were to cover only a five-year span. They decided they did not want to send out messages which confirmed the status quo of the time. Instead, they actually decided to stick with the TGAT framework as it stood and explained that one reason for doing this was to lay the ground for a possible future time when teaching of MFL would begin before the age of 11: 'The desire not to make modern languages look different from other foundation subjects and the possibility of future modifications which might encourage modern language teaching to begin at a younger age than that specified in our terms of reference were also powerful motives.' (Department of Education and Science [DES], 1990.)

They also pointed out specifically that they believed that the reason full-scale teaching of MFL in primary schools was not happening had little to do with a clear rationale and everything to do with the lack of suitably trained and qualified teachers. In making this point they echoed an earlier statement from Her Majesty's Inspectorate of schools (HMI), that: 'There is no one correct age at which to begin to learn a foreign language. For largely practical reasons, however, such as the supply of suitably qualified teachers and continuity between phases, it is generally around the age of 11...' (DES, 1987: 28.) It is interesting to note that in this same earlier statement HMI observe that: 'Receiving schools need to take account, in both their organisation and their teaching, of what incoming pupils have encountered and achieved..'

This observation strongly suggests that an important lesson from the flawed Burstall *et al* (1974) research report a dozen years earlier had actually been learnt by those stalking the corridors of power in English education, even if the logical consequence, that therefore shutting down the primary French experiment on the basis of the Burstall Report was unjustified, has never been officially admitted. The positions of both HMI and the NCMLWG, expressed in documents published through government channels, nevertheless indicated a degree of embryonic official support for an idea which had been pretty much dismissed throughout the previous decade. Behind this dawning shift there might just possibly have been the glimmer of realization that the Burstall report might be ceasing to be a reasonable basis on which to continue opposition to the idea of pre-11 teaching of MFL.

These might be called signs of hope from the top. As will become clear though, the hope of resurrection for primary MFL through a top-down development of policy was actually to prove if not actually illusory, at least disappointing, as the 1990s progressed. Much more important in the event have been the signs of hope and real growth emerging in the opposite direction. From the late 1980s onwards there were unmistakable indications that the teaching of primary French and other MFL was making a comeback despite the lack of overt official policy. Several local authorities and some individual schools began to take 'unilateral action' and implement their own policy on primary MFL in a clear 'grass roots', 'bottom-up' movement. Early players in the field included authorities such as Tameside in Manchester with its PRISM scheme, Kent with the scheme which was eventually published as *Pilote* (KETV 1992) and the heroic East Sussex, which had battled on against the odds throughout the 1970s and 1980s and continued to provide peripatetic French teaching across the county for all Y6 pupils. It eventually published its scheme, *Salut La France*, in 1989, although unfortunately the LEA reached a point in 1997 where it felt it could no longer bear the costs of county-wide provision and peripatetic teaching was ended.

Around 1990 there developed a national pre-11 languages network organized originally by Ron Adelman from Tameside and then taken on by Peter Satchwell who at the time was modern languages inspector for Surrey, where 10-year-olds in middle schools were being taught French. This organization has continued throughout the 1990s to provide a forum for all those interested in the provision of MFL teaching to children in the primary age range, and it has gone from strength to strength. It has regular meetings now attended by teachers, teacher-trainers, advisers, inspectors, academics, and policy makers numbered in dozens. It is now playing a key role in helping the Blair government to take forward its 'serious consideration' of primary MFL. From little acorns...!

By 1992 two major national associations were beginning to become involved. The Association for Language Learning (ALL), the national organization of teachers of MFL, and the National Association of Headteachers (NAHT), the principal national organization of primary headteachers, staged a joint conference entitled 'Primary Foreign Languages – A Fresh Impetus'. Both organizations had 'become increasingly aware through their own membership of a growing interest again in the learning of foreign languages by children of primary school age' (Trafford, 1994: 4). The conference was told that '25 local education authorities across the country have schemes in place or some element of foreign language teaching in the primary sector' (Trafford, 1994: 6). The unstated government view at the time was reported by Lady Brigstock, who was a member of the House of Lords European Committee. This amounted essentially to 'waiting a few years for the new National Curriculum to be established when every 16-year-old will have studied at least one language from the age of 11 and there will be a larger pool from which to gather the necessary supply of primary school teachers who are competent enough and confident enough to teach a language'. In the meantime she said that the government 'would positively encourage any primary school that did teach a language'. Lady Brigstock distanced herself from this official view and gave positive encouragement to the two associations to 'get down to specific planning' because 'now is the time'.

This the associations did in the form of two parallel very positive statements of policy. The NAHT policy was based on a resolution passed at its annual conference in 1992 which called on the government to make 'progress towards the introduction of foreign language learning before the age of eleven', to bring in 'the requirement of a foreign language qualification as a condition of qualified teacher status', and to establish 'a major programme to train teachers of foreign languages'. The opening sentence of the ALL policy was the firm declaration, 'This Association strongly supports an early start to the study of modern foreign languages.' It went on to contend that 'Foreign language learning could begin at any age before 11, but our immediate aim should be the introduction of foreign language learning in Key Stage 2 of the National Curriculum in England and Wales', and that 'plans need to be laid now to enable the properly co-ordinated development of foreign languages in the primary phase'. It supported the same range of measures advocated by the NAHT. Interestingly, the ALL policy concludes with a direct reference to the injustice of provision being made in the private sector but not in the state system. 'The privileges enjoyed by the minority must be extended to all.'

Although these forceful declarations from powerful organizations had no discernible effect on the government of the day, they did provide rallying points for the onward movement of the grass roots primary MFL bandwagon. By 1996 a survey by the Centre for Information on Language Teaching (CILT) was able to report that around a third of all pupils moving from primary to secondary schools had been taught a foreign language in one way or another.

In one part of the UK, however, the British government was acting in an entirely different manner. From 1989 onwards the same government which refused to commit itself to the early teaching of MFL in England was actively promoting the subject north of the border. Michael Forsyth, Scottish minister for education, published Circular 1178 of the Scottish Education Department which proposed a 'languages for all' policy extending teaching down into the primary years. It has to be acknowledged that the parallel with the situation in England is not exact. Transfer occurs a year later in Scotland and so beginning MFL in the secondary school already meant a later start. However the circular proposed more than just making up the additional year. While educational arguments were advanced in support of the policy, especially the need to prepare young people to take advantages of the coming into force of the Single European Market in 1992, there were also political motives relating to the position of the governing Conservative Party in Scotland at the time. Its popularity was ebbing and there was a feeling that the introduction of primary MFL would be popular with parents. As Low (1999) points out, it is no coincidence that several of the first six pilot projects, which were centred on secondary schools working together with their feeder primaries, were located in the relatively small number of Scottish constituencies with

Conservative MPs. So popular did the pilots prove that the Conservative Party in Scotland went on to promise in their manifesto for the 1992 General Election campaign that they would extend the policy to all primary schools and that there would be universal primary MFL teaching by 1997.

Given the bottom-up pressure from local initiatives in England and a completely anomalous situation in another part of the UK it is arguable that the primary MFL renaissance was becoming unstoppable as the 1990s progressed. With government spokesmen seemingly willing to put forward contradictory arguments depending on whether they were talking about Scotland or England, while at the same time fiercely advocating equal and uniform entitlement in an imposed National Curriculum for England, it could not be long before some regularization of the situation would occur.

Underpinning developments in the renaissance of primary MFL

Within the professional MFL teaching community substantial changes had taken place in the final quarter of the 20th century which were to have profound implications for the position of the subject in relation to primary education. Over a period of two decades or so there was a major shift in the predominant philosophy of modern language teaching in general, amounting in effect to a change of paradigm (Kuhn, 1962). The prevailing emphasis moved from earlier preoccupations with grammar/translation approaches through a period where audio-visual approaches rooted in behaviourist psychology predominated to a much greater concern with communicative competence as both method and objective. This 'paradigm shift' was 'officially' signalled in the 1987 HMI document referred to above, which asserted that: '[This document] takes as its guiding principle that learning a foreign language should be primarily a matter of learning it for communication... Maximum exposure to and involvement in spoken and written language within the pupils' grasp are the basis of effective learning.' (Kuhn, 11.)

The role of the teacher was now seen as creating a situation for pupils in which they could use the foreign language for real purposes to communicate meaning: 'Those activities which enable genuine communication to take place or which simulate it closely are the most effective. Such opportunities as are provided by the necessary business of the classroom should be fully exploited, for example counting and spelling, noting absence, apologising, introducing people, asking permission and requesting an explanation.' (HMI, 1987.)

Once modern language teaching became essentially concerned with fostering communicative competence significant primary MFL opportunities were opened up. Indeed it could be argued that there was a certain irony in the fact that primary schools, which were not statutorily required by the provisions of the National Curriculum to teach MFL were, by virtue of their form and organization, much better placed to deliver a programme of communicative competence than the secondary schools which are actually charged with it (Sharpe, 1991). Table 1.1 proposes an analysis of the contrasting teaching situations in the two types of school intended to demonstrate this point.

Table 1.1   Teaching at primary and secondary level

Issues	Primary Level	Secondary Level
Children	Own class – 30 pupils	Different classes – 100+ pupils
Professional obligation	General	Specific
Role of the teacher	Multifaceted	To teach defined content
Educational aims	Broad	Determined by subject
Classroom organization	Informal	Formal
Ambience	Communal	Focused
Timetable	Flexible	Fixed

(Source: Sharpe, 1991: 50)

Even now, despite all the changes which have been made in the regulations governing primary education, and all the rhetoric about the importance of specialist and semi-specialist teaching at Key Stage (KS) 2, it is still the norm for the primary class teacher to spend all or most of each day with 30 or so children, having a general all-round responsibility for their development as well as usually teaching more or less the entire curriculum range. Although notions of catering for 'the needs of the individual child' and promoting the development of the 'whole child' were during the 1980s and 1990s relentlessly subjected to what Ball (1992) has called a 'discourse of derision', it remains the case that primary teachers are expected to promote the physical, social, cultural, moral and spiritual development of children as well as their cognitive and intellectual growth. In this endeavour they inevitably establish deep relationships with pupils whom they see all day everyday for a period of at least a year, and in the case of small schools several years. Indeed this 'deep relationship' is necessary for the very 'general' professional obligation professional teachers have towards their pupils. It would be difficult to see how they could fulfil the kinds of expectations of them implicit in monitoring and promoting such all-round development if they did not really know their pupils thoroughly and personally. Given these very broad educational aims, it is unsurprising that the role of the teacher in the primary classroom becomes very diverse, and multifaceted, with times of direct instruction, exposition and questioning in a whole class context, but also times of facilitating group and individualized learning, even autonomous and self-directed learning, where the teaching role is altogether lower profile, less overt and less visible. Since the report of the 'Three Wise Men' (Alexander, Rose and Woodhead, 1992) it has become fashionable to talk about 'fitness for purpose', to say that the primary teacher has a repertoire of teaching styles and strategies which can be drawn on, and that the choice of a particular approach must be justified with reference to the particularities of the lesson objectives and the nature of the children being taught.

Broad flexibility in teaching style is matched by comparative freedom from the constraints of a rigid timetable. This of course varies according to the size of the school, but generally speaking the number of fixed points in the primary school teacher's day which are outside his or her control is relatively small. These are made up of set school times, such as start and end of school time, lunch-breaks and playtimes, although even here individual class teachers may have some choice. Then there are the facilities of the school, such as the hall, perhaps the games field, or a specially equipped room for say science and technology or ICT, which all have to be formally timetabled to enable provision to be shared between classes. There may be timetabled setting arrangements for core subjects and 'exchange' arrangements for subjects such as music. But for most of the time when the primary class teacher is with his or her own class, he or she has a high level of scope for autonomy in deciding when to teach what. This remains the case even though the pressures from the outside have grown in recent years, with National Curriculum programmes of study impinging on content, and more recently government schemes such as the literacy and numeracy hours beginning to encroach on methods. The Dearing review of the National Curriculum in the mid-1990s and the lifting of the requirement to teach the programmes of study of the foundation subjects in 1998 have restored some of the traditional autonomy which primary teachers felt had been threatened during the early 1990s. More recent developments, such as the new less prescriptive National Curriculum, which took effect from September 2000, arguably lead this process on a stage.

Primary teaching still takes place largely in the context of an informally organized classroom with a communal atmosphere which tends to create a powerful sense of belonging. How very different is the typical secondary school teaching situation, where teachers face a succession of different classes, maybe in a succession of different rooms, with the specific obligation to transmit defined content within a defined period of time. Whereas the primary school classroom is a continuing community in which, at least for the school day, the whole of life is lived, the secondary school classroom is more of an ephemeral association for a particular purpose. Even with the literacy and numeracy hours which prescribe pedagogic activity as much as curriculum content, the fact still remains that both are mediated through the general class teacher's relationship with his or her pupils. At its extreme it could be argued that the difference between being a pupil in the primary classroom and in a secondary classroom is analogous to the difference between family life and attending a meeting.

Paradoxically the logic of this argument is that actually the primary school that is not obliged to teach MFL is a more conducive environment in which to make progress in communicative competence than the secondary school which has the statutory demand placed on it. Secondary pupils are well aware that the French (or other language) lesson is given in isolation and is not coordinated with other subjects or systematically related to other aspects of school life. Even if the room in which say French is taught genuinely recreates the atmosphere of France, pupils spend only a fraction of their time in it. It is much more difficult for them to perceive the foreign language as a natural means of communication when their overwhelming experience of schooling reinforces English cultural perspectives, English social assumptions and, most significantly, the English language. Primary schools on the other hand are institutionally structured to facilitate the permeation of the foreign language across the whole curriculum and in every aspect of school life. Within his or her own classroom the primary teacher can ensure that all the ordinary routines of everyday life are carried out in French: taking the register, collecting dinner money, lining up, writing the date, celebrating birthdays, setting the weather chart, distributing books and folders and so forth. The teacher can use French as the medium for all regular classroom commands: 'Sit down', 'Line up', 'Get out your books', 'Write the date', 'Be quiet', 'Put your hand up', 'Wait there', 'Come here', etc. As well as teaching specific MFL lessons the teacher can integrate French into the teaching of all other subjects in ways suggested in the discussion of the National Curriculum and primary MFL in Chapter 3. And none of this requires unrealistically high levels of linguistic knowledge. Much of it can be learnt easily and then assimilated quickly through constant and familiar repetition. For the children this makes French a real part of themselves and their lives. The foreign language becomes routine, habitual and unremarkable. Through their close relationship with the primary teacher young children trust the meaningfulness of non-English structures and vocabulary. They are of an age to be taken along by a committed and enthusiastic presentation without the vulnerable self-consciousness of adolescents. The foreign language is in this way 'normalized'.

Embedding French language and culture in the primary child's whole school experience in this 'global' manner was in fact how the original 1960s government pilot project discussed earlier actually began, with the work of Mrs M Kellerman in Leeds cited in the Schools Council publication in 1966. Her success was attributed at the time to the fact that she took every opportunity to use French as the means of communication in all aspects of her teaching. It is arguable that this integrationist view was overshadowed as experts committed to the then dominant behaviourist paradigm took over writing the scheme of work used in the project, and attention was directed towards structured drills and lexical progression. Teachers involved in the mid-century project were not trained to operate like Mrs Kellerman. Now that the emphasis is on communication this original insight can be recovered. It is important to be clear that embedding a foreign language in the way outlined does not itself constitute a method of teaching. Foreign language learning is radically different from mother tongue acquisition and there is always a need for systematically planned direct teaching and progression. What matters, however, is that teaching within an integrationist environment transforms the significance for pupils of what is learnt and can potentially raise standards of achievement and motivation. Where this approach is shared by the whole school and has the support of the school's senior management the benefits can be magnified, and the process can begin at a very early age. In the Ecole Maternelle du Phare in Calais, France, three-year-olds are given regular lessons in English and do much of their ordinary classroom work in English. Their teachers talk of *le droit au bilinguisme* and believe that their efforts to embed the foreign language in the lives of these very young children are a response to a fundamental entitlement.

The move to communicative competence then has turned modern language teaching into something which fits the primary school context well. This contemporary pedagogic approach also resonates with many long-established basic canons of good primary teaching methodology, a point which will be developed throughout this book. Alongside this educational factor in the re-emergence of primary MFL which has been mediated through teachers and other educationists, other more external factors have played an important role. The build-up to the 1992 establishment of the Single Market obviously affected England as much as Scotland and the preparations raised awareness of the opportunities and challenges which young people would face in the Europe of the future. Many parents realized that their children would be disadvantaged in relation to their counterparts in other member states of the Union if they did not learn at least one foreign language and acquire 'European' attitudes. The debate about Europeanization intensified throughout the decade. At the same time there has been a growing recogni-

tion of the phenomenon of globalization which generates the same imperatives on a world scale. Increasing mobility in occupations as well as foreign
travel for holidays and leisure have weakened traditional views of the significance of boundaries of all kinds, including national frontiers. Electronic
communications, and especially the Internet and the World Wide Web, have
given an added impetus to the sense that the world really has become a global
village. The changing social attitudes that these sociopolitical and technological processes have engendered have underpinned a greater demand by
parents for primary schools to teach a foreign language. Headteachers,
governing bodies and local authorities have had to respond to this demand.

Thus in the early years of the 21st century the context in which the debate
about the place of MFL teaching in the early and middle years of schooling is
taking place differs radically from the mid-century conditions in which the
first national project was conceived. At the time of writing it remains to be
seen whether the encouraging prime-ministerial statement quoted in part at
the beginning of this chapter will eventually be translated into concrete
action to provide primary MFL teaching for all. However, momentum for this
has gathered. In arguing now for the place of MFL teaching at primary level
we need to consider what educational aims and objectives the subject can
now be said to achieve, and this is the focus of Chapter 2.

2

Aims and objectives of primary MFL teaching

The contribution of MFL teaching to education

What is it that justifies the place of foreign languages in schooling? Why is the learning of a foreign language regarded as an educational experience? Many other kinds of learning are not seen as educational and not included in the ordinary school curriculum, gardening or learning to play cards for example. Across the world there is now virtually universal agreement that foreign languages should be taught in schools, so prima facie there is clearly a strong case to be made.

In practice it is possible to view the contribution that foreign languages can make to education in two distinctly different ways. The first line of argument is that by acquiring knowledge of and skill in a foreign language the learner gains access to the rich store of uplifting and edifying literature written in that language. This is essentially the reason the ancient languages, Latin and Greek, were included in the school curriculum of the 19th century, and when modern languages began to be recognized as legitimate areas of study in schools during the 20th century the same kind of rationale was often advanced. One should study Latin to be able to read Homer, and one should study French to be able to read Molière or German to read Göethe. Behind this approach lay the notion of the 'educated man', passing on to the next generation what it was necessary for them to know to be regarded as members of the educated classes. (There was of course in the 19th and early 20th century little real concept of the 'educated woman' in this sense, and still less of the 'educated person' irrespective of gender). This is education seen as a particular type of culture, what we might now call 'high culture'. The job of schools was to transmit this culture, which was seen as having a self-evident intrinsic value. Reading the ancient classics or the modern European classics was regarded as an uplifting experience in its own right. It improved the mind. It did not need to be justified with reference to anything else. For this reason it seems fair to call this type of justification the *'intrinsic' justification*. It is this kind of justification which underpins what was described in Chapter 1 as the essentially 'idealistic' culture historically of the independent preparatory and public schools.

Throughout the 20th century, however, an entirely different approach to justifying the teaching of modern foreign languages emerged, which arguably has now overshadowed the intrinsic justification. The study of dead languages necessarily carried with it the implication it could never lead to direct communication with native speakers of those tongues. While even up to the 20th century doctors and Roman Catholic priests might use Latin in the normal course of the exercise of their professional duties, there was clearly no chance of them or anybody else ever being able to have an ordinary conversation with a living Roman for whom Latin was the mother tongue. Looking back now it does seem extraordinary that few people seemed at the time to notice that French, German, Spanish and other European languages increasingly being taught in schools were different in this crucial respect. Pedagogic and curricular methods used in teaching Latin tended to be simply transferred across to the teaching of MFL. It was not really until the mid-20th century that the idea of teaching MFL primarily for the purpose of enabling learners to communicate with native speakers gained widespread acceptance. Once accepted, however, the way was open for a much more *'instrumental' justification* for the inclusion of MFL in the school curriculum, grounded more clearly in the kinds of 'utilitarian' criteria for determining originally what should and should not be taught in elementary schools, as discussed in Chapter 1. It now became more common for advocates of MFL teaching in schools to base their arguments on the idea that it is useful to be able to speak other languages because one can then communicate with native speakers directly rather than through the medium of interpreters. The instrumental justification for MFL is linked to a more general change in attitudes to the purposes of education. Discussions of what education is, and is for, have come in recent decades to be marked by a much more utilitarian approach which focuses upon the social and economic benefits which it is supposed to bring. In the case of MFL the discussion is often couched in terms of businessmen and salesmen talking to international customers and 'clinching deals' because of their ability to speak the language and thereby form direct personal relationships. It is of course often said that for native English speakers the instrumental argument is much less strong because English is a world language understood pretty much everywhere now. On the surface this seems a reasonable position, but it may also be true that in economic terms there are still advantages in being able to communicate in the home language of clients and customers. The observation by a late 20th century German politician that he was always pleased to talk with his British colleagues and friends through the medium of English but that if any of these colleagues and friends wanted to sell him or his countrymen some particular goods or services, *dann müssen sie Deutsch sprechen!* (then they'd better speak German!), neatly captures the point.

These two justifications thus focus on contrasting views of what education is all about, and to some extent represent competing ideologies that have struggled with each other throughout the past hundred years during which national universal education systems have been institutionalized in all advanced industrial societies. Some of the main parameters of this ideological conflict are suggested as the answers to five basic questions as shown in Table 2.1.

Table 2.1 Main parameters of intrinsic (idealistic) and instrumental (utilitarian) cultures

	Intrinsic (idealistic) culture	Instrumental (utilitarian) culture
The **Why** question: What is education for?	To preserve and transmit high culture	To promote economic, social and individual benefit
The **Who** question: Who is education for?	Elite/selected groups	Mass population
The **When** question: What time period should education be oriented to?	The past	The future
The **What** question: What is education about?	That which is traditionally accepted as worthwhile, good, true, beautiful, etc.	That which is useful
The **How** question: How should education be delivered?	Through teacher-centred didactic teaching	Through learner-centred active learning

Gradually the rationale for the inclusion of any subject in the school curriculum has moved from emphasizing the intrinsic answers to the basic questions to a stress on the subject's contribution to the instrumental answers. In the case of MFL this has meant underlining the need for high levels of linguistic knowledge and skill in the population at a time in history when there is ever greater mobility, social and geographical, and ever expanding opportunities for rapid communication and exchange, including of course the mind-boggling possibilities for global intercommunication opening up through the Internet and the developing World Wide Web. The perceived need to club together in order to 'compete' in the global marketplace is leading to the emergence of groupings of nations with different language traditions. The EU is a clear example not only of closer integration on economic grounds but also of integration driven by politicians concerned to eradicate old enmities and hostilities. The intention is that barriers to mobility of all kinds should be broken down. However, so long as any language barriers remain it cannot really be said that other barriers have been fully dismantled in actuality. Thus the usefulness of MFL lies in its contribution to the achievement of cross-national fluidity and the full realization of the opportunities this new regime offers to individuals. Speaking of the importance of multilingualism for individuals at a Council of Europe conference in Strasbourg in 1997, Domenico Lenarduzzi, European Commission Director of Education said:

> This is not a mere wish but an absolute necessity. Without sufficient linguistic knowledge there will be no mobility, no dialogue and no understanding... Each citizen should be in a position to know two other languages. If young people do not have languages they will be confronted by discrimination... Whether we like it or not, all our member states must make efforts to adapt their teaching.

The kind of discourse this gives rise to in the political realm tends to take as axiomatic that there is 'need' for foreign language skills as part of an education which prepares children for adult life in a world increasingly dominated by multinational organizations and enterprises. These organizations pay little regard to national frontiers and expect their employees to have the ability and confidence to operate in languages and cultures different from their mother tongue and home culture. To the extent that this 'need' is not being met it is feared that business is still being 'lost'. By ensuring that the need for foreign language capability is addressed, education systems can be seen to be discharging their responsibilities in an appropriate manner for the prevailing historical circumstances. In this way the benefits to the collective – the nation, the EU, or 'society'– on the one hand, and the benefits to the individual on the other, are seen to coincide. The collective is more harmonious, more efficient and more successful, while the individual realizes her or his full potential, achieves employment and career success, and is presumably as a consequence more fulfilled and happier.

This may all sound like what has sometimes been sneeringly dismissed as 'social engineering'. However, it is important to recognize that in its nature any education is always inescapably an act of social engineering in so far as it inevitably involves the intentional moulding and changing of individual human minds in defined social contexts. In the 19th century, in schools whose rationale was essentially 'intrinsic' as described above, there was a very real intention to form a particular kind of person. In England this in many instances took the form of producing, or perhaps more correctly, reproducing the 'gentleman', in each succeeding generation of pupils. What distinguishes the intrinsic and the instrumental approaches is not that one 'engineers' and the other does not, but rather that in one case the engineering is designed to reproduce trusted models of the past while in the other it is specifically aimed at producing something new which will be better adapted to the future.

A corollary of the inevitability of social engineering in any education system is that all schooling shapes individuals' sense of who they are. In the past it was certainly arguable that the way MFLs were taught, ie as if they were dead languages like Latin, meant that they simply reinforced the effect of the other subjects of the curriculum in creating a particular kind of national identity. In history lessons pupils would learn about the great glories of the nation into which they were born, in literature lessons they would read about the insights and thoughts of previous great and good countrymen, in team sporting activities they would relive the values and moral beliefs of their forbears, 'play up and play the game' for example, in the English context. And then if they were taught French or Spanish or German it would be presented to them largely as some kind of linguistic code of English through mastery of which they might access yet more European great thoughts and insights. It did not fundamentally challenge their own ingrained cultural assumptions about the social world of their own everyday life. I vividly remember as a teenager going to France in the 1960s after four years studying French and being utterly astonished that real live human beings actually spoke this language for real, mundanely, naturally, 24 hours a day.

We understand much more fully now the ways in which language and culture interact as inseparable elements in a constant symbiotic relationship. We understand the relativity of language. There is no one given, correct way of labelling things. Ralph Wightman, a frequent panellist on the old BBC Home Service radio programme *Any Questions*, during a broadcast in the 1950s once famously observed that while the Germans call it 'Wasser', the French 'eau', and the Italians, 'acqua', the Englishman with all his good, down-to-earth common sense, calls the stuff water, which is of course obviously what the stuff really is.

Whereas in reality, of course, it isn't. One of the strong instrumental arguments now being used for advocating the importance of MFL teaching is precisely that in the future everybody will need to understand and come to terms with this realization. We all now need to feel comfortable stepping outside the comforting womb of monolingualism. Monolingualism is that cosy and reassuring illusion that one's own mother tongue is really the only proper way of bringing the world alive, that chimera which leads many to feel sympathy with views such as the one so neatly expressed by that great English eccentric Quentin Crisp, 'the naked civil servant', who declared, 'I don't hold with abroad and think that foreigners speak English when our backs are turned'. In the conditions of the third millennium the monolingual world will increasingly be revealed for the deceptive mirage that it has actually always been. When languages and their underpinning cultures were relatively insulated from each other monolingualism could remain a hard social reality for most people. In conditions of high mobility and the dissolution of linguistic boundaries people need to be able to feel at ease in more than one culture and the language through which it is expressed. In order to achieve this it is necessary that MFL teaching not only fosters linguistic skill but also develops in pupils a solid empathy for the culture in which the particular language is embedded. MFL teaching needs to challenge ingrained prejudices and stereotypes about the people and the culture of the target language which pupils may have acquired from their home culture. In other words MFL teaching is being asked to take on the role of confronting rather than confirming the pupil's home culture. Pupils need to be made not just multilingual but multicultural too. A major reason in the 21st century for teaching MFL in schools is the contribution it can make to citizenship education in the form of tolerance towards multiculturalism in the home society and a willingness to embrace multilingualism and multiculturalism in the wider world. More generally, MFL teaching is expected to assist in developing in young people a positive attitude to human diversity. In England, MFL teaching is increasingly being seen as having a major contribution to make towards the development in pupils of a sense of their European citizenship. This issue is explored in some depth in Chapter 5.

Since the late 1980s there has been in England a real preoccupation with aims and objectives in educational debate. While both aims and objectives are concerned with setting out to achieve some predefined end state, the difference between them is one of level and scale. Aims may generally be considered as higher-level intentions on a broad scale. Objectives are usually regarded as more limited in scope and specific in intent. The educational reforms of the late 1980s and 1990s were concerned with redefining the aims of education, and in terms of the above discussion it can be said that overall policy has centrally focused on moving English education from intrinsic answers to the five basic questions to more instrumental themes. At the same time pressure has been put on those professionally engaged in the English education system to identify appropriate objectives in order to achieve the higher-order aims established as official policy.

The impact of all these reforms on MFL teaching has been mainly to downplay as aims the significance of any mind-enhancing qualities supposedly inherent in the process of studying foreign languages and reading elevating foreign literature, and at the same time to seek ways to provide opportunities for all school pupils to have access to MFL learning opportunities. Objectives implicit in activities such as syllabus setting and lesson planning have been required to be much more focused on what has come to be termed communicative competence.

The concept of communicative competence

The fundamental intention in pedagogic approaches focused on communicative competence is quite simply to equip the learner with the knowledge, skills and interpersonal strategies they need effectively to be able to communicate with speakers of the language in question. The concept of communicative competence is at the heart of the philosophy now institutionalized in the National Curriculum's programmes of study for MFL.

> Pupils should be taught... to develop their independence in language learning; use their knowledge to experiment with language... develop strategies for dealing with the unpredictable. (DfEE, 1995: 3)

> Pupils should be taught... how to initiate and develop conversations, how to vary the target language to suit context, audience and purpose and strategies for dealing with the unpredictable. (DfEE, 1999: 16)

Communicative competence is both the means and the end; learners are taught to communicate through communicating in lessons.

In contemporary discussion about MFL teaching it has become a sine qua non that teaching should take place in and through communication in the foreign language. It is though possible to argue that there are strong and weak versions of communicative competence. The strong version says that because the aim is the development of competence in communicating in the target language all teaching should ideally be delivered through the medium of that language. This, Brumfitt (1995) suggests, is the 'mood of the national curriculum', which has put an obligation on (secondary) MFL teachers to use the target language as near as possible to 100 per cent of the time in MFL lessons. It is arguable, however, that there is some ambiguity, if not confusion, over means and ends. It is not prima facie obvious why the task of equipping learners with communicative competence is invariably best achieved by talking to them always in the target language. From the teacher's point of view the 'weak' version of communicative competence might be that, given what is actually involved in facilitating the development of communicative knowledge, understanding and skills, a percentage of lesson time always needs to be given over to instructions and explanations in the pupils' mother tongue. At a basic level of effective time management many teachers might argue that to spend a lot of time repeating things in the foreign language and waiting for the pupils to 'deduce' what is being meant is to waste the small amount of time they have actually to teach the subject. Far better, they would argue, to give a quick explanation in English and move on. Such teachers would contend that the 'weaker' form of communicative competence is more efficient teaching. That grand old gentleman scholar of language teaching Eric Hawkins famously suggested that teaching MFL is rather like 'gardening in a gale' where the few seeds of MFL knowledge the teacher–gardener is able to plant are always at risk of being blown away from the continuous gale that is the mother tongue of the home culture used in all circumstances other than the foreign language lesson. He is though adamant that this does not mean that some explanations are not better given in the learner's mother tongue for the sake of expedience: 'to banish the mother tongue is to tie the teacher's hands wastefully' (Hawkins, 1987: 175).

In short a balance needs to be struck between maximum exposure of pupils to the foreign language and the most efficient use of limited MFL teaching–learning time. This balance is illustrated in the two forms of communicative competence shown in Table 2.2.

Table 2.2 Balance of use of target language in two forms of communicative competence

	Strong	Weak
Teacher usage	Maximum use of target language	Judicious use of target language
Learner outcome	Creative use of target language for own purposes	Effective communication in target language in defined circumstances

When to use the strong or the weak form of communicative competence in actual teaching situations is a matter for the professional judgement of individual teachers. The degree of ambitiousness in terms of longer-term intentions defined as learner outcomes is similarly a matter for course planners in their particular circumstances. Broadly speaking, from the point of view of teachers, it is clearly easier for those with high levels of skill in the language being taught to use the strong form, employing the language flexibly and spontaneously with the ease of native or near-native speakers, while those whose level of skill is more modest, such as non-specialist primary teachers, might use the weak form in the sense of limiting themselves to specific areas of 'comfort' in the language linked to the syllabus themes and topics. In relation to learner outcomes, the strong form is essentially about producing speaker-listeners/reader-writers in the target language who can function in a manner approximating more or less that in which they operate in their home language. The weak form aims at enabling learners to operate efficiently in particular situations, often now defined in terms of social functions such as describing oneself, asking the way, buying things in shops, booking hotel rooms, etc.

In practice, however, the difference is less clear cut. Even teachers who have native levels of skill will sometimes find it expedient to use the learners' mother tongue to explain things which it would simply take too long to get at in what to the learners may be incomprehensible foreign language utterances. Never using anything but the target language can result in inefficient learning. At the other end of the spectrum, with good teaching, there is no reason why even limited programmes and curricula should not encourage some creativity on the part of learners. I was once with a group of English primary school children on a day trip to Calais. At a supermarket one child was having difficulties with the extensive collection of comestibles she had garnered from the shelves, and she said to the checkout assistant, 'Donnez-moi un sac plastique, s'il vous plait'. This was not a sentence she had ever heard before. She had created it from her understanding of three bits of language, the structure, *donnez-moi*, the vocabulary of nouns and adjectives, and the conventions of politeness.

Even at quite low levels therefore having learners take control, or 'ownership', to use the preferred jargon of the times, of the language they are learning is essential to the idea of communicative competence. Communicative competence is often taken these days as a self-evident term. In point of fact, however, it is used in different ways and covers a range of teaching–learning activities. What these activities share in common is that they are grounded in a particular sociolinguistic conception of what it means to 'know' a language. In this view there are various components of competence which together constitute the ability to speak any language. Understanding these components is useful to teachers in enabling learners to become 'communicatively competent' in the target language. Canale (1983) identifies these in the following way:

- grammatical competence (linguistic competence, narrowly defined – pronunciation, syntax and vocabulary);
- discourse competence (knowledge of the rules governing the structure of longer texts, conversations, etc);
- sociolinguistic competence (control of speech and writing styles appropriate to different situations, knowledge of rules of politeness, etc);
- strategic competence (knowledge of coping strategies which can keep communication going when language knowledge is still imperfect – eg how to negotiate meaning or repair misunderstandings).

It is useful to bear in mind these separate aspects of communicative competence because it has sometimes happened that just one has been assumed to be the only real aim of modern language teaching. In the past it has, for example, been assumed that grammatical understanding itself constituted more or less alone the sole purpose of modern language teaching. It is only necessary to examine the French primers used in English schools in the mid-20th century to see the parallel with Latin primers of the same era and thereby detect the extent to which the two languages were seen as constituting similar kinds of academic exercise for pupils. I have vivid memories of reciting verbs of the various conjugations: first, second or third in Latin; –er, –ir, –re in French, and seeing the activity as much the same in both cases. *Amo, amas, amat, amamus, amatis, amant, je porte, tu portes, il/elle porte, nous portons, vous portez, ils portent*, stay with me to this day, some 40 years later. While both my French and Latin teachers were insistent that I should learn to spell these conjugated verbs correctly (more difficult in French of course where you cannot 'hear' some of the changes), I have little recollection of anybody every worrying that I might be able to use them to express my own meaning or make sense of the culture of ancient Rome or contemporary France. The link between *porter* as an infinitive exemplar of *–er* verbs and *porter* as a linguistic tool to use in functioning effectively in French-speaking countries was never made apparent to me in French lessons. To be fair, other approaches to teaching Foreign languages may be charged with similar narrowness. Some of the audio-visual methods of the 1960s and 1970s focused so exclusively on the drilling of appropriate responses to given situations, based as they often were on the 'stimulus–response' theories of the behaviourist school of psychology, that they committed the same error of mistaking a part for the whole, treating the appearance of sociolinguistic competence, the seeming ability to say 'the right thing' in particular circumstances, as if it amounted to communicative competence.

What then is meant by each of the elements of communicative competence?

Grammatical competence

Grammatical understanding is the ability to formulate and comprehend sentences and other acceptable utterances which accord with the fundamental rules of grammar built in to the language. Chomsky long ago showed us that human infants have an apparent innate capacity to learn grammatical rules very quickly. He pointed out that other theories of how children learn, such as behaviourism, cannot really account for the speed with which young children assimilate the grammatical structure of a mother-tongue language. There simply is not time for them to experience enough language to learn the rules without having already in place what he called a 'language acquisition device' (Chomsky, 1965). It is really quite remarkable how secure the grasp of two- and three-year-olds actually is on the fundamental structures underpinning their mother tongue. The mistakes they make clearly demonstrate this knowledge. When a toddler declares, 'yesterday I swimmed in the sea', what he or she is showing is a clear understanding that in order to indicate an action which happened in the past 'ed' must be added to the verb.

Discourse competence

Marrying together an appreciation of the linguistic/grammatical rules and the social/cultural rules governing language use requires a particular type of conversational skill which can usefully be encapsulated in the idea of discourse competence. There are particular kinds of vocabulary and language structures associated with discussing, say, financial matters in a bank, or dealing with medical staff in hospital after an accident, or conversing with other guests over a meal at a dinner party. These distinctive forms of 'language-in-use' constitute specific discourses. It is not enough simply to know the grammatical and sociocultural codes; the communicatively competent speaker-listener needs to be able to manage themselves correctly in actual scenes of social interaction. Native speakers have particular ways of conducting themselves in the context of these discourses and to become really communicatively competent foreign language learners need to acquire the same skills and capacities if they are ever to aspire to 'pass' as competent members of the target language community.

Sociolinguistic competence

It is vital also to know the broader social and cultural context in which native speaker-listeners 'live' the language. Of the myriad of possible grammatically correct things that could be said, native speakers in any language only actually say a small fraction. Learners need to know what natives typically say in typical situations. It is a not uncommon human experience to hear foreigners who have mastered the linguistic rules of a language perfectly and have managed to develop near perfect accents nevertheless starkly reveal their non-native origins by constructing sentences which sound alien to natives' ears. The Frenchman who wishes his English hosts 'good appetite' at the dinner table blows his cover. The Englishman in France who through a feeling of Anglo-Saxon repugnance at the idea of bodily contact cannot bring himself to shake hands or kiss when greeting, and who treats tu and vous as if they were both equally good and always interchangeable equivalents of 'you', is likely to fail to be really communicatively competent and risks upsetting people. The US businessman who has graduated from an advanced Japanese class but who tramples all over Japanese society's sociolinguistic rules of modesty, reserve and social etiquette will not secure many contracts. The communicatively competent speaker of a language needs to be familiar with, and sensitive to, the cultural setting in which that language is embedded. For in that cultural setting there lies an intricate web of taken-for-granted knowledge and tacit understandings about what is and is not appropriate, right and proper in any given social encounter.

Strategic competence

This competence underpins the above three and essentially consists in knowing how to manage social interactions in the target language and culture, including the ability to open and close conversations, understanding role expectations in conversations such as turn-taking, knowing what to do when communication breaks down, knowing how to seek clarification of something not understood, dealing efficiently with 'gaps' in knowledge, employing avoidance tactics, and the like. All those pragmatic social and linguistic skills are needed when the foreign language is being used in the real situation by someone who has learned it artificially rather than naturally and who is faced with the need to overcome difficulties in communicating caused by their incomplete knowledge of the language.

These four elements then are at the heart of what most foreign language teaching nowadays aims to achieve. The last point is particularly significant, as it is always important to bear in mind that the kind of communicative competence which MFL teachers are aiming to produce in learners can never be precisely that which exists between native speaker-listeners of the target language. For the second-language learner there will always be a degree of artificiality in the communicative competence acquired. Byram (1999) has developed a similar analysis around the concept of 'intercultural competence' to emphasize the need for MFL teachers to recognize that their work is directed to 'artificial' rather than 'natural' communicative competence. In particular he draws attention to four *savoirs*:

- *Savoir être* – attitudes. The learner needs to acquire a positive interest in the target language and culture. He or she needs to notice what is going on, positively seek to find out more about people of the culture, and accept different behaviours as normal and not simply reject them as alien.
- *Savoir* – knowledge. The learner needs to know what to do in the language, to be familiar with different expectations and habits, to understand the different ways of doing things in the target language and culture.
- *Savoir comprendre* – skills of interpretation. The learner needs to be able to apply understanding of the cultural background in making sense of utterances and documents. This means going beyond mere translation to an appreciation of the significance of particular language events. Byram gives the example of reading a school report and not simply translating it word for word but understanding its implications in the context of an understanding of the education system in the country concerned.
- *Savoir apprendre / savoir faire* – skills of discovery and interaction. The learner needs to develop skills of enquiry about what is taken for granted in the target language and culture. There will always be things that are treated as self-evident and not said with which the MFL learner is unfamiliar. Skills are needed to elicit these.

Thus at the heart of teaching communicative competence is the intention of the teacher to change the learner's personal experience and ways of dealing with the world. Speaking a foreign language means experiencing one's self and one's surroundings differently. The foreign language learner is required to change his or her identity and turn into a foreigner, a stranger, an outsider, who has to get to grips with the environing social world anew. All the familiar, easy and comfortable props of the mother tongue and culture are gone and absolutely fundamental relearning about basic taken-for-granted realities has to take place. As discussed in Chapter 1, for the most part, as far as MFL teaching in schools is concerned, pupils do not embark on this daunting process until the secondary stage of education which they usually start at the age of 11. Increasingly, however, this state of affairs is being questioned, both within the UK and elsewhere.

Six main aims of primary MFL teaching

The main reason why there is so much discussion now about beginning the learning of foreign languages in the primary phase of schooling is that once it is agreed that the main purpose of teaching foreign languages is to equip learners to be communicatively competent, as described above, it can be argued that there are some clear advantages in beginning the process before the age of 11. There are six main aims associated with the idea of early teaching of foreign languages to young children:

● To exploit the linguistic and cognitive flexibility of primary-age children (the 'young learners are better learners' argument).
● To exploit the attitudinal and motivational flexibility of primary-age children (the 'young learners are more eager and malleable learners' argument).
● To raise levels of achievement through learning (possibly more) languages for longer (the 'higher standards' argument).
● To exploit the opportunities presented by the particular circumstances of the context of primary schooling for promoting language awareness and second language acquisition (the 'primary context advantages' argument).
● To provide young children with an important and enriching experience which will better equip them to understand the realities of life in the third millennium (the European/global citizenship 'entitlement' argument).
● To equip the next generation with the requisite knowledge, skills and understanding which will enable them to function effectively in international contexts (the 'social and economic benefits' argument).

Young children and language acquisition

There is a widespread common-sense assumption that because young children learn their mother tongue so quickly and efficiently they can similarly effectively learn a second language. This of course ignores the huge gulf that separates the two experiences. On the one hand is the human experience of acquiring a first language (L1) through which young children come naturally to understand who they are and through which they establish fundamental relationships with parents and family and begin to make sense of the world around them. On the other is the artificial contrived encounter with a foreign tongue (L2) and an alien culture in a formally organized teaching situation. First and second language learning are just not the same kinds of activity. Children cannot be expected unproblematically to transfer the learning skills from the former to the latter.

The other major idea underpinning the 'young is best' approach is that there is some kind of 'optimum age' to learn foreign languages. This idea became popular around the middle of the 20th century and essentially proposes that there is a 'critical period' during which children are especially amenable to language acquisition. Such an approach was congruent with many other developmental theories which were fashionable at the time, including the 'stages of development' thesis. While in common-sense terms it may seem reasonable to suppose that young children are more malleable and that before puberty the brain may be more flexible and adaptable, there is actually little in the way of conclusive research to support this type of theory. And of course the critique of Piaget's whole theoretical edifice is now well established (Donaldson, 1991).

It has to be acknowledged that this is one of those questions where research findings across a wide range of disciplines simply do not build up into a very clear picture. There is some evidence that actually older learners learn more efficiently. Oller and Nagato (1974) found that older beginners make much more rapid progress than younger learners in primary school. Burstall *et al* (1974) also found that there was no noticeable superiority in reading and writing in those who had had three years of primary teaching, although, as already indicated, this research has been heavily criticized. There is also the optimum age argument: this says there is a period in early childhood when conditions are optimized for language acquisition. The only evidence to support this is in studies of language learning situations which are 'naturalistic' rather than 'scholastic'. In particular the 'French language immersion projects' in Canada (Lapkin, Hart and Swain, 1991) appear to succeed better in the case of pre-school children than those who start at the age of 10. There appear to be some specific benefits in relation to the ability to imitate sounds accurately (Vilke, 1988; Low *et al*, 1993). The Scottish primary modern languages project found that pupils who had learnt MFL in the primary school showed a greater readiness in the secondary school to answer orally and were more likely to use longer and structurally more complex utterances, they under-stood more language discourse, and were 'more able to accept sustained foreign language input' (Low *et al* 1993: 132).

But from research and evaluation studies of the same Scottish project Johnstone (1994) reported definite advantages apparent amongst older learners:

- better general learning strategies;
- better grasp of grammatical patterns and rule in language;
- more practice in negotiating and sustaining conversations;
- more defined purpose in learning the language;

● greater knowledge of concepts, eg time, which can be transferred to the new language.

Johnstone, however, also points out that in this kind of research it is simply not possible to control all the variables needed to make fair, accurate and equitable comparisons between young and old learners. It is actually also diffi-cult to test differential learning outcomes between older and younger learners since on the whole tests favour older candidates. For example, there are certain inescapable cognitive demands inherent in the process of translation, and younger learners' failure to perform may merely reflect their less devel-oped cognitive powers rather than indicating failure to learn aspects of the foreign language. In the 1996 Reith Lectures, Jean Aitchison again argued for the advantages of starting early:

> The idea of a critical period (for mother tongue acquisition) is now disputed...
> Yet most people find it easier to learn languages when they are young, so a sensi-
> tive period may exist... A 'natural sieve' hypothesis is an idea put forward to
> explain this. Very young children may... automatically filter out complexities...
> Later learners may have lost this built-in filter... A 'tuning-in' hypothesis is
> another possibility. At each stage a child is naturally attuned to some particular
> aspect of language. Infants may be tuned in to the sounds, older children to the
> syntax, and from around ten onwards the vocabulary becomes a major concern.
> Selective attention of this type fits in well with what we know about biologically
> programmed behaviour. (Quoted in Hawkins, 1996: 157)

In 1987 Singleton observed that second-language acquisition research is not 'an abundant provider of answers' and it has to be acknowledged that this situ-ation remains largely unchanged at the beginning of the third millennium. As Johnstone has recently noted: 'On developmental grounds each age in life probably has its peculiar advantages and disadvantages for language learning... in the sixties the mistake was made of expecting miracles merely by starting young. The miracles have not come about. Starting late, as such, is not the answer either' (Quoted in Hawkins, 1996: 158).

With his extensive experience of the study of early modern language teaching, Johnstone nevertheless concludes that on balance the available evidence supports the value of an early start in primary schools.

Young learners' motivation

While it may be difficult to show clearly that young children are more effi-cient learners of foreign languages, it is perhaps less difficult to argue that on the whole they are easier for teachers to motivate. Furthermore, young children may be much more receptive to the broader aspects of foreign language learning, such as developing a positive attitude to difference and diversity, understanding multilingualism and the relativity of language, and accepting European and global citizenship values. Once more it has to be acknowledged that there is little in the way of hard evidence, and therefore we have to rely on what seem reasonable propositions. But in the attitudinal sphere this may be more compelling than in the clearly more 'technical' area of capacity for language acquisition, given that it appears to parents, primary school teachers and the general population that it is easier to impact on pre-11 children than it is on adolescents.

Now that language learning is based on the fostering of communicative competence the question of motivation has become crucial. This is a subject where teachers really do have to face up to the dictum that 'you can take the horse to water but you can't make it drink'. Unless the learner is motivated to communicate there really is not much point in trying to teach a foreign language. In the old 'grammar-translation' days pupils could be made to do written exercises, but it is impossible to make someone 'want' to engage in conversation. Primary teachers tend to be skilled motivators, and the material they are working with is more plastic than if they were teaching older pupils. Not only this, but primary-age children are in general likely to be much less self-conscious and reticent in front of their peers when it comes to being asked to make the funny sounding noises of the new language. The case might be therefore that in the primary school pupils start to learn a foreign language in a supportive and enjoyable context, as a result of which they develop positive feelings about foreign language learning in general which colour their attitudes and behaviour subsequently in the secondary school. In this sense the early start is seen as a kind of immunization against later negative attitudes which might emerge after puberty.

If it is agreed that younger learners are easier to influence in terms of their feelings, attitudes and values than older learners, then the other, non-linguistic, key aims and objectives are arguably more effectively achieved with an early start. Teachers seeking to promote tolerance and cross-cultural understanding through MFL work in their classrooms may find more fertile ground among pre-11 pupils than post-11 pupils, whose prejudices, albeit assimilated from the parental home, the media and the general cultural background, may be more firmly established and consequently more difficult to challenge. Linked with this is the need to ensure that pupils have a proper understanding that they live in a multicultural, multilingual society which is a member state of the multicultural, multilingual EU, which is itself part of an increasingly globalized world community. A corollary of recognizing the multilingual character of the social environment is the understanding that one's mother tongue is only a human language and not *the* human language, however widely it happens to be spoken.

MFL is the subject par excellence which is seen as contributing to the growing child's understanding of the importance of valuing diversity. While it again can be said that confronting these kinds of issues in the secondary class-room is made more manageable by the greater capacity of older learners to articulate and reflect on ideas, there seems prima facie nevertheless to be a stronger case here for believing that the bright open-mindedness and exuberant enthusiasms of young children can and should be harnessed to the establishment of these ideas in prepubescent heads. In so doing it can be claimed that the early teaching of MFL makes a significant contribution to what in the English national context is called personal and social education (PSE) and spiritual, moral, social and cultural education (SMSCE), as well as laying the ground for more responsive learning of MFL in the later stages of education.

Raising standards by learning languages longer

Here too it would seem to the average person on the proverbial Clapham omnibus to be only common sense to imagine that starting earlier and there-fore spending more time on language learning will improve results at the end of the process. In principle more time means more exposure, more opportu-nity to practise and more chance of gaining mastery. In practice this only really works if it is true that young learners learn languages efficiently. If they do not then the argument is weakened. An important part of the rationale for the Kent scheme (Rumley and Sharpe, 2000) was the planners' intention that primary MFL teaching would enable earlier completion of the secondary syllabus with the possibility of a) better overall results in GCSE MFL and b) starting a second language earlier. There is some anecdotal evidence that stan-dards have been raised in this way, but no systematic research evidence is yet available.

It could be that it would be better to spend additional time on MFL learning in the secondary school when pupils have acquired greater skill in using learning strategies generally. This view would accord with those who wish to see a greater concentration on 'the basics' in the primary school, the argument being that if pupils acquire basic skills before the age of 11, these skills can then be utilized after 11 to underpin more sophisticated styles of learning across a range of subjects and disciplines. Given the differences in learning styles then between younger and older learners, it is not by any means self-evident that more time spent learning MFL at the primary stage would necessarily produce higher levels of linguistic proficiency. In the

NFER study (Burstall *et al*, 1974) the researchers reported that secondary pupils who had not learnt French in the primary school tended to 'catch up' quickly, and certainly by the age of 16 there seemed to be no difference in general levels of attainment between those who had learnt French at primary school and those who had not. However, as has already been pointed out, there were a number of serious problems with this research and the findings about 'catching up' may just as well reflect the fact that the secondary schools did not build upon knowledge acquired by the pilot children during the primary years. It is though noteworthy that it appears to be only in the field of MFL that anyone seriously pursues the argument that it is not worth primary schools teaching anything because pupils can catch up later. Nobody says primary pupils should not be taught multiplication tables or anything else in mathematics because they could learn them much more quickly later. Yet the same arguments surely apply. It is possible that in much of the discussion about primary MFL, and arguably much of the research, there is an a priori unconscious acceptance of the status quo of starting at age 11.

Since the advent of the National Curriculum it has been abundantly clear that the early stages of MFL learning could, if there were sufficient trained teachers, easily be delivered in the primary school. This was made explicit from the first deliberations of the NCMLWG a decade ago, a point discussed in Chapter 3. In the present situation where teaching officially begins at 11 there is actually a mismatch currently between MFL content and the age of learners. Primary pupils would match this early content much better. One possible development in the longer term might be that much teaching material currently provided at KS3 might be delivered at KS2, and this would similarly provide for KS4 material to be delivered at KS3. In this way the subject could 'slip down' a Key Stage, which would have the tremendous advantage of capitalizing on the markedly positive attitude of pupils aged 7–11 and avoiding the debilitating and demotivating consequences for both teachers and pupils of having to confront the more negative attitudes of many pupils aged 14–16. Positive-minded KS4 pupils could opt to take their MFL studies further and thereby achieve higher standards at 16 than they would otherwise have done. The rest could opt out, but the overall content of programmes of study would have been delivered at an optimal period from the point of view of pupil attitudes, and in this sense the MFL standards of all pupils would have risen and a sound base for later MFL learning in adult life would possibly have been established.

For the time being, however, there is no such national plan, and it is important for local initiatives to include clear provision for continuity and progression from whatever is done in the primary school to feed into more demanding expectations from the beginning of secondary schooling. It also does seem reasonable to expect an overall gain from providing primary pupils with better attitudes to foreign languages and cultures, and a heightened awareness of languages. In present circumstances, it is probably in this way that the main contribution of primary MFL to raising eventual standards of MFL achievement at the end of secondary schooling is actually being most effectively made.

Advantages of the primary school situation for language learning

The primary school context provides a better learning context for MFL than the secondary school. The committed primary generalist teacher can significantly reduce the force of Hawkins' mother-tongue 'gale' and is potentially therefore a more effective 'gardener' than his or her secondary counterpart. The primary teacher can do this by *embedding* the foreign language in the child's whole school experience and by *integrating* it into the whole primary curriculum on top of the systematic teaching provided. Providing that primary MFL teaching is properly sensitive to the distinctive ethos of primary schools it can be delivered successfully and effectively. This is the central message of this whole book. The final report of the Council of Europe Workshop 8B states: 'The need is for teachers who are specialists both in primary education and foreign language pedagogy. As primary school experts they will be familiar with the conditions and the framework into which, as foreign language experts, they can integrate the language and culture of other countries.' (Quoted in Driscoll and Frost, 1999: 146.) The concepts of embedding and integration were discussed in Chapter 1 and will be explored throughout all of the remaining chapters of this book.

Wider benefits young children derive from language learning

The main benefits young children derive from learning MFL are those to do with understanding the diversity of human and languages and cultures. This understanding has both intrinsic and extrinsic benefits. Intrinsically, it is arguably an entitlement of all children that they should be given this understanding, which enhances and enriches their conceptions of themselves and their world as human beings living in the third millennium. They have a right to be emancipated from the fallacies of monoculturalism and monolingualism. Extrinsically it is also very useful because without open attitudes and intercultural competence young people will not be able to take advantage of the opportunities which now lie before them. They will need the communication skills to be able to move with ease and confidence from one country to another, and to interact with people from all over the world through electronic media. Xenophobia and racial prejudice are not only inherently reprehensible, they are also a severe impediment to the full realization of individual potential in the world of the 21st century. There are also considerable benefits to pupils' progress in other subjects of the primary curriculum and to their mastery of oracy and literacy in general, a point to be developed further in Chapter 3.

Social and economic benefits of primary MFL teaching

These are the flip side of the individual benefits outlined above. All nation states need to come to terms with the consequences of globalization. The business world is no longer much constrained by national frontiers and increasing numbers of people are employed in multinational enterprises. Within the EU the political intention is to make a reality of the Single Market in which there is unfettered mobility. More than half of UK exports go to non-English speaking countries, but without appropriate language skills and multicultural attitudes business will struggle to sustain and develop this position. The European Commission White Paper (1996), 'Teaching and Learning: Towards a learning society', declares that:

> Languages are the key to knowing other people... it is becoming necessary for everyone... to be able to acquire and keep up their ability to communicate in at least two Community languages, it is desirable for foreign language learning to start at pre-school level. It seems essential for such teaching to be placed on a systematic footing in primary education, with the learning of a second Community language starting in secondary.

For all the above reasons it is clear that there are good grounds for believing now that an early start to the teaching of MFL will improve overall performance in the subject, and thereby contribute to the political agenda of raising standards.

Language acquisition in primary MFL teaching

There has been some discussion in the literature about how ambitious the overall aims of primary MFL should be. Much of this has arisen out of the debate in France over whether the concern in primary schools should be with *sensibilisation* or with *apprentissage*, which can be roughly translated as sensitization or acquisition. Essentially this revolves around the issue of whether primary teaching should aim actually to begin the process of helping pupils to acquire a foreign language and gain a specific level of proficiency in a single target language, or whether what matters most is that pupils should be sensitized towards the existence of foreign languages in general, laying foundations which will facilitate acquisition at a later stage.

In practice this is something of a false dichotomy. There is an obvious sense in which all good teaching in the primary school involves sensitizing pupils to the nature of language in such a way that they develop an awareness of the roots and origins of words, the diversity of linguistic forms, the essential functions and structures of language in general. Sensitization understood as 'language awareness' (Hawkins 1984, 1987) is really not much more than what primary schools should be doing anyway. At the same time, of course, raising language awareness is an important spin-off of the systematic teaching of MFL in primary schools where it is provided. Labelling a primary MFL scheme as just offering 'language awareness' is sometimes a tactic used by MFL purists who seek to criticize approaches based on the use of generalist teachers and who see the only 'real' primary MFL teaching as that delivered by 'expert' specialist teachers.

Good MFL teaching aimed at raising standards can be provided in primary schools by either generalists or specialists. This issue is discussed further in Chapter 6. The key point is whether there is a clear intention to deliver a planned and systematic programme of instruction in a foreign language to primary-age pupils, however ambitious or modest the aims and scope of that programme, accompanied by a clear intention that gains in linguistic mastery thereby achieved will be recognized and built upon in subsequent teaching in the secondary school. Once there is clearly organized planned teaching there is a commitment to *apprentissage* or language acquisition, which will also bring in its wake a heightened sensitization to languages in general and to cultural differences.

The recently issued non-statutory guidelines for modern foreign languages at KS2 of the National Curriculum make no distinction between sensitization and acquisition. They contend that the contribution the subject makes to the primary curriculum is both linguistic and cultural:

> The learning of a foreign language in primary school provides a valuable educational, social and cultural experience for all pupils. Pupils develop communication and literacy skills that lay the foundation for future language learning. They develop linguistic competence, extend their knowledge of how language works

and explore differences and similarities between the foreign language and English. Learning another language raises awareness of the multilingual and multicultural world and introduces an international dimension to pupils' learning, giving them an insight into their own culture and those of others. The learning of a foreign language provides a medium for cross-curricular links and for the reinforcement of knowledge, skills and understanding developed in other subjects. (DfEE, 1999: 32)

This inclusion of primary MFL in the Year 2000 National Curriculum is a highly significant development which is explored in Chapter 3.

Part 2

The 'what and when' issues

3

Primary MFL and the National Curriculum

Background

The Education Reform Act of 1988 introduced a National Curriculum for the first time in the history of education in England and Wales. Concern about the inadequacies and inequities arising from the differences which existed between the curricula provided by different schools in different parts of the country had been expressed since the mid-1970s. Prime Minister James Callaghan's famous speech at Ruskin College in 1976 launched the 'Great Debate' on education which led to the whole package of reforms instituted by the Conservative governments of the late 1980s and early 1990s. The conception underlying any national curriculum is that every child has a basic curriculum entitlement which should be delivered by whichever school the child attends in whichever area the child lives. The only grounds on which this fundamental entitlement should in any way be varied are in the case of a pupil with defined special educational needs; after 1988 the vagaries of 'local variation' were ended. In the years since the Act was passed the form and content of the National Curriculum has changed many times, but the essential core idea that it consists of a set academic subjects to be taught in all schools remains. Another constant factor is that the only subject which is required to be taught in secondary schools but not in primary schools is a modern foreign language.

At the time when the National Curriculum was being set up there was much discussion about whether modern languages could be taught in the primary school. This was the period during which many local projects run by LEAs and by individual schools had begun to experiment with schemes to introduce a foreign language in some way into the primary curriculum. The Working Group established by the secretary of state for education to draw up the National Curriculum for modern languages suggested that the early teaching of modern languages was in principle a good thing but observed that: 'Full scale teaching of foreign languages in primary schools... is not at present possible, not because children of this age cannot successfully learn a language but because very few teachers in primary schools are equipped to teach it'. (DES 1990: 5.)

To a considerable extent such an assertion is still dependent on the assumption that high levels of linguistic mastery in teachers are a necessary prerequisite for anything worthwhile to be achieved with primary-age children. One of the purposes of this book is of course to question the validity of this assumption. From 1990 onwards evidence emerging from local projects, the national project in Scotland and the experience other countries has clearly indicated that generalist primary teachers can be trained to deliver effective programmes of modern language teaching without having to pursue lengthy and costly courses of linguistic instruction. Indeed, in the years following the MFL Working Group's pronouncement so successful were the unplanned and unintended local primary MFL projects that in a major review of the whole National Curriculum undertaken in 1993 by the Dearing committee (which recommended that approximately 20 per cent of curriculum time should be freed up) specific mention was made of the subject: 'to teach optional content outside the statutory core of each subject and for non-National Curriculum work where appropriate (for example for the introduction of a foreign language at Key Stage 2 where the school has relevant expertise)' (Dearing 1994: 82).

On the face of it this does seem an extraordinary sequence of historical development. Firstly, the government introduces a common curriculum entitlement to overcome the unfairness and the perceived economic inefficiency of pupils' not all being taught the same things. This specifically, and uniquely, excludes the teaching of a modern language in primary schools. Then, despite all the difficulties and the enormous pressures on schools and teachers arising from implementing a National Curriculum, which by 1992 virtually everyone agreed was overburdened and unwieldy, schemes for primary modern language teaching arise phoenix-like (Sharpe, 1991) in a bottom–up movement to a large extent driven by parental desire to a point where between 30 and 35 per cent of pupils entering secondary schools had experienced some form of foreign language provision (McLagan, 1996). Next the government moves to deal with the unmanageability of the National Curriculum by 'slimming it down', so that it now constitutes only four-fifths of the total teaching time available, and at the same time specifically suggests that the 'free-floating fifth' might be used in primary schools to teach the one subject it had directly excluded from the primary curriculum!

In connection with this strange turn of events two well known French phrases spring readily to mind: *déjà vu* (non-literal translation: we've seen this before) and *plus ça change, plus c'est la même chose* (non-literal translation: the more things change the more they stay the same). For in truth this position with regard to primary modern languages and the National Curriculum is a replay of the general situation before the National Curriculum existed. The inequities have returned. What possible justification can there be for the provision of modern language teaching to pupils in Canterbury but not in Cambridge, in Edinburgh but not in Exeter? Of course it is arguable that the whole post-Dearing 'slim' version of the National Curriculum itself represented a return to the status quo ante of official encouragement to diversity in educational provision, but that is another topic which would take us far beyond the question of modern languages in the primary school. After Dearing a five-year moratorium on change in the National Curriculum was announced so that reform-weary teachers could consolidate their teaching programmes without endless modifications, adaptations and alterations in curriculum content. The key question for advocates of primary MFL was whether the 'throw-away' 'for instance' from the Dearing review quoted above actually heralded a change in government thinking about the early teaching of modern languages which would result in some kind of inclusion in the post-moratorium National Curriculum for the next millennium.

At a conference on the place of modern languages in the primary school organized by the Schools Curriculum and Assessment Authority (SCAA) its then chief executive, Dr Nicholas Tate, firmly declared that: 'SCAA has no views on the future role of modern foreign languages in the primary school. We approach the issue with an entirely open mind.' (SCAA, 1997: 7.)

In 1997 it was already difficult to see how such a stance could be maintained in the longer run. Primary MFL teaching was happening even before Dearing, and Dearing clearly gave a degree of positive encouragement to its further development. In this way all the factors creating an impulse towards its renaissance discussed in Chapter 1 were pushing at a door which if not open was at least now ajar. The problems associated with this haphazard emergence (or, strictly, re-emergence) of primary MFL were inevitably going to grow, and eventually it was to be expected that a point would be reached where politicians and policy-makers would perceive that 'something needs to be done'. When this happened decision-makers would be faced with having to decide either to support it or to discourage it. Given the strength of feeling about this on the part of the different stakeholders involved, especially parents, the latter option had become all but impossible. For this reason advocates of primary MFL increasingly took the view that it would be only a matter of time before some further action was taken. In the event they did not have to wait anything like as long as some imagined.

Primary MFL and the revised Year 2000 National Curriculum

Almost as soon as Dr Tate had declared his view that the principal authority for curriculum development in England had no view about the place of MFL teaching in primary schools, planning began on the future form and content of the National Curriculum which would come into force after the moratorium to take effect from September 2000. On 25 March 1999 the under secretary of state for school standards, Charles Clark, announced a new government initiative from the DfEE 'to promote and develop the provision and quality of Modern Foreign Language learning in the Primary sector', which would be coordinated through the Centre for Information on Language Teaching and Research (CILT).

This really was quite a surprising turnabout in the official position on MFL teaching in English primary schools. For a couple of years Ofsted had been using guidelines for the inspection of MFL in primary schools which offered the subject and wished their work in the field to be included in their inspection. This was taken to imply a degree of official recognition, if not approval, of the actual position that nationally there were by the late 1990s significant levels of provision. The guidelines were short, limited to one side of A4, but nevertheless this was the first time that any government-linked body had adopted a formal stance on the matter.

Clark's announcement, however, was of an entirely different order. Here was a government spokesperson directly proclaiming a U-turn on previous policy. The decade of the 1990s had opened with the unplanned re-emergence of something officially believed to have been extinguished in the 1970s, and something which it was felt in government circles by and large should stay extinguished. By the mid-1990s the best that could be said was that there was official indifference, at most neutrality, on the still growing renaissance of primary MFL teaching, and then suddenly, in the final year of the decade, a seismic shift towards official encouragement and support.

The objectives identified for the new initiative were:

- To provide advice and support for institutions involved in or considering the provision of early MFL learning.
- To offer greater support and coherence for existing initiatives.
- To support networks for sharing experience.
- To establish a basis for future developments.

These objectives would be principally achieved through two specific actions. Firstly, there would be established a National Advisory Centre on Early

Language Teaching (NACELL) to be based at CILT. It would become the main vehicle through which advice, support and coherence would be coordinated. There had been in existence since the late 1980s a primary modern languages network which met twice a year and brought together enthusiasts from schools, LEAs, teacher-training institutions and research organizations. For a number of years this had been based at CILT. NACELL would build upon this and other less formal and less national networks, and in so doing make particular use of information and communications technology (ICT). It would coordinate the development of further high-quality curriculum materials and multimedia resources for teachers and seek to disseminate models of good practice. This was to include a review of training for teachers of MFL in the primary sector.

Secondly, there was to be a 'Good Practice Project' in which bids would be invited from schools and LEAs to receive a small amount of funding to support pilot primary MFL projects to be reported on in developing further guidelines. Of the 64 bids, 18 schools and LEAs in England and Wales were selected to contribute to a project which worked to identify, develop and disseminate good practice in primary MFL. It ran from September 1999 to March 2001 and provided advice to the Qualifications and Curriculum Authority (QCA), which replaced the SCAA. Interim findings were made available to the QCA in September 2000 to enable it to produce official guidelines to support the introduction of the revised Year 2000 National Curriculum with the non-statutory guidance on teaching MFL at KS2. The official documentation posted on the World Wide Web (www.nacell.org.uk) notes that this project was intended to 'help to prepare the ground for the wider introduction of MFL into the primary sector should the government wish to change current policies at some point in the future'. The same Web site published Issue 1 (May 1999) of a periodical entitled *The Early Language Learning Bulletin* in which the Director of CILT, Dr Lid King, warned that 'We must, of course, be clear that this does not mean the introduction of Modern Languages as a statutory part of the Key Stage 2 curriculum'.

Nonetheless the publication in late 1999 of the revised National Curriculum to take effect from September 2000 may come to be seen as a landmark in the history of primary MFL teaching in England. While throughout the whole set of Year 2000 National Curriculum subject documents the all-pervading theme is one of pruning content, taking the Dearing principle explained above still further, paring down the specific requirements of the programmes of study and the attainment targets, suddenly the teaching of MFL at KS2 appears as a new entry, an additional element which seems to run counter to the whole ethos. It is one thing to have government ministers beginning to make more positive noises, it is quite another to have a whole section of the National Curriculum document for MFL given over to guidelines, albeit non-statutory, on introducing the subject at KS2. Their mere presence would seem to stand as an official endorsement of the principle. Schools and LEAs might be expected to feel more and more pressured to offer the subject to pupils. It is difficult to explain to parents why their offspring should be denied primary MFL teaching when pupils elsewhere are receiving it, and it is explicitly provided for within National Curriculum documentation. This innovation has changed the context within which the debate about modern languages in the primary school is now held.

Renewed impetus has in this way been given to the whole primary MFL movement. Feedback from NACELL and the Good Practice Project was used by the QCA to draw up more detailed advice and exemplar schemes of work to assist primary schools teaching MFL. These were published in Autumn 2000, and inevitably seem to imply further official approval of the activity.

The National Curriculum MFL content

The inclusion of non-statutory guidance for MFL at KS2 is not the only striking feature of the post-2000 National Curriculum. Another notable aspect is just how much it has been reduced to a shadow of its former self. The actual programme of study for MFL as a specialist subject at KS3/KS4 now comprises just two pages. The bulk of the rest of the 48-page document is given over to generic statements about the structure and organization of the National Curriculum as a whole. Strictly speaking it might now be argued that the new millennium National Curriculum is not a curriculum at all, in the sense that a curriculum is supposed to define substantive content. With only 4 per cent of the surface area of its pages actually referring to 'what pupils should be taught', and most of this in fact on closer scrutiny concerned with *how* rather than *what* they should be taught, the document appears as more in the way of a methodological text than a detailed curriculum per se. The vast majority of the MFL document consists of standardized pages and paragraphs about the National Curriculum in general which are repeated in every single separate subject document.

Further analysis of the brief programme of study itself reveals a marked lack of specificity that minimizes still further the 'curricular' force of the requirements. Much of it is pitched at such a high level of generality that it is difficult to see how one could engage in any act of MFL teaching and not automatically comply. To say, for example, that pupils 'should be taught correct pronunciation and intonation' or 'should be taught to ask and answer questions' is really not to say much at all. It is the MFL equivalent of commending 'motherhood and apple-pie'. One might ask what else would an MFL teacher be doing?

The form of the MFL programme of study is a list of items comprising: 'knowledge, skills and understanding', which are to be taught through nine defined activities described as Breadth of Study. These two categories are standard constituent features of the programmes of study for every subject. The knowledge, skills and understanding items are grouped under four headings:

● Acquiring knowledge and understanding of the target language.
● Developing language skills.
● Developing language-learning skills.
● Developing cultural awareness.

The various elements listed under each heading are focused very much on processes rather than prescribed content as such, for example 'techniques for memorising words, phrases and short extracts' or 'considering their own culture and comparing it with the cultures of the countries and communities where the target language is spoken'.

The Breadth of Study section is similarly concerned with content-free procedures rather than defined content, for example 'expressing and discussing personal feelings and opinions' or 'listening, reading or viewing for personal interest and enjoyment, as well as for information'. The limited scope of the post-2000 National Curriculum contrasts sharply with the much more detailed MFL National Curriculum document which preceded it. In these circumstances the earlier version is likely to continue to influence classroom practice. The areas and activities it listed reflected a broad consensus about what needs to be covered in the subject. As such, it is useful for primary teachers embarking on KS2 schemes of work to be familiar with prevailing ideas about the form and content of teaching at KS3.

The defined content is divided into two parts: 'learning and using the target language', and 'areas of experience'. The first part is further subdivided into four sections which have been more or less retained in the revised Year 2000 version. They are described as:

● communicating in the target language;
● language skills;
● language-learning skills and knowledge of language;
● cultural awareness.

What is interesting for present purposes about the lists of prescribed activities which follow each of these headings is the extent to which they correspond with long-established features of effective primary practice. They continue to testify to the principle enunciated by the MFL Working Group which, after having stressed the value of visual display, practical demonstration and active learning, observed that 'this is one of the many areas in which teachers of foreign languages can learn from good primary practice' (National Curriculum Council, 1990, para 6.17). To illustrate this the section dealing with 'communicating in the target language' is analysed below to demonstrate the 'transferability of skills' in MFL teaching which is part of the successful primary teacher's professional repertoire. This analysis draws attention to the relative ease with which committed primary teachers can incorporate modern languages into the curriculum they offer their pupils. In relation to communicating the target language, for example, the rubric requires that pupils should be given opportunities as follows.

To communicate with each other in pairs and groups, and with their teacher.
Primary teaching involves using a variety of groups and forms of classroom organization to achieve the range of pedagogic and curricular objectives appropriate to the age range (Sharpe, 1997). In particular, primary teachers work with the concept of 'fitness for purpose' described earlier (Alexander, Rose and Woodhead, 1992), in which promoting fruitful communication between pupils in pairs, small groups and whole class situations is a key consideration. Experienced primary teachers are aware of the vital importance of providing young children with the opportunity to articulate their thoughts, discuss issues and practise skills in both pupil–pupil situations and in pupil–teacher interaction in all areas of the primary curriculum. Pair work and group work are at the heart of promoting and reinforcing learning in primary MFL.

To use language for real purposes, as well as to practise skills.
Because in the early and middle years of schooling children are still in the process of learning about their world, and learning the language through which that world can be described and talked about, all good lessons at the primary stage of education in whatever subject need to provide the pupil with clear and appropriate language through which what is being learned can be expressed. It has long been a sine qua none of primary teaching that it is better for the teacher to structure lessons in such a way that children use written and spoken language for real purposes rather than simply to meet the limited demands of arid, decontextualized exercises. At the same time it is also recognized that children need opportunities to practise skills such as handwriting, careful pronunciation and so forth, and getting the balance right is a professional judgement with which good primary teachers are very familiar.

To develop their understanding and skills through a range of language activities, eg games, role play, surveys and other investigations.
In the post-war era primary education has given a major place to active learning as a fundamental underlying principle of good practice. In all subjects of the primary curriculum good primary teachers seek ways in which children's knowledge, understanding and skills can be deepened through involvement in contextualized activities in which the language of history, art, geography or whatever to which they have been introduced can be 'naturally' applied, practised and consolidated. Games and role plays are the main means through which primary MFL are taught.

To take part in imaginative and creative activities, eg improvised drama.
The development of children's powers of creativity and imagination has been a major concern in primary education in both senses of the word. The 1967 Plowden Report on primary education more or less gave pride of place to developing each child's unique individuality through creative exploration and discovery as the best way of promoting learning and development. Throughout the 1980s and 1990s anxious concern has been expressed that because of this emphasis insufficient attention has been paid to formal instruction and direct teaching (Alexander, Rose and Woodhead, 1992). Primary teachers in the late 1990s were thus very aware of the value of allowing children opportunities for creative self-expression within an overall programme providing for a 'balanced diet' of learning modes.

To use everyday classroom events as a context for spontaneous speech.
This is 'meat and drink' to the primary class teacher, who knows the value of exploiting the ordinary routines and happenings of classroom life to support ongoing teaching. As suggested in Chapter 1, the primary teacher is actually better situated than the secondary specialist teacher of modern foreign languages to draw on the rich seam of real shared collective experiences since he or she is with the children the whole time. The linguistic benefits which can accrue from this situation are discussed throughout this book. The concept of spontaneous speech needs to be understood sensitively. Young second language learners, primary or secondary, can never emulate the spontaneity of speech in the mother tongue. Spontaneity in this sense tends to mean something along the lines of encountering a situation in which it is realized that earlier learned language can be appropriately used. Seen in this light primary teachers can promote this, and do so in a wider range of circumstances than the secondary MFL teacher, who 'lives' with any one cohort of pupils for only brief specified periods of time.

To discuss their own ideas, interests and experiences and compare them with those of others.

Here too we are in the field of fundamental primary strategies. The starting point for many lessons, both in creative areas and in more focused substantive areas such as history, for example, will often be a discussion of the children's own feelings, memories, experiences, views, opinions etc. This inspires motivation and commitment and can give pupils a sense of participation and ownership in their learning processes. Equally, using their experiences at other stages in a lesson is a common approach, drawing together, for example, what pupils have been doing in mathematical or scientific investigations in order to facilitate comparisons, contrasts, conclusions. In the context of MFL this might mean using French or other languages to compare likes and dislikes, for example.

To listen, read or view for personal interest and enjoyment, as well as for information.

The above words describe key primary aims in the teaching of reading and the promotion of children's speaking and listening skills which are at the heart of effective learning in all subjects of the curriculum. Primary MFL needs to be experienced by pupils as fun and enjoyable, and the listening and reading activities involved need to motivate pupil engagement. Even at the primary level children can be exposed to a range of reading material for different purposes. In other subjects, such as mathematics pupils can use information presented in French or another language to draw out data, for instance tourist leaflets to research statistics on weather or distances. There are well-established projects using newspapers in different languages from which, by using knowledge of context and genre, young children can still elicit substantial chunks of information from text written in unfamiliar words.

To listen and respond to different types of spoken language.

The development of pupils' listening skills is a key aim of primary teaching. Primary teachers routinely engage in activities designed to heighten children's awareness of, and sensitivity to, the variety of forms of speech, and to teach them the importance of matching their own spoken language appropriately to the audience concerned. Primary MFL activities commonly include listening to authentic voices in order to identify key facts such as age.

To read handwritten and printed texts of different types and of varying lengths, and where appropriate, to read aloud.

Again, as an aspect of the teaching of reading this is clearly central to everything which primary teachers do. In relation to MFL at both primary and secondary level this is clearly more constrained than is the case in English. But

even at primary level it can involve looking at real books, perhaps of traditional fairy tales and accompanied by a taped reading, or of pamphlets and
leaflets, or of short directed letters from pen friends in a partner school,
which, provided they keep to taught and known language structures, could be
read aloud.

To produce a variety of types of writing.
Equipping pupils with the skills needed to be able to write for a range of
different audiences is one of the main objectives of primary teaching. Even
though great care needs to be exercised in teaching writing in primary MFL,
most teachers believe that some writing should be undertaken. This could
take the form of writing signs (in French, for example, *sortie, entrée, bienvenue,
toilettes*, etc), or controlled letters to pen friends. In relation to the civilization
aspects, linking with geography, history, art or music, for example, children can
clearly produce a variety of types of writing in English.

To use a range of resources for communicating, eg telephone, e-mail, fax, letters.
Primary teachers have a responsibility for including information and communications technology (ICT) in lessons across the curriculum. ICT is now an
integral part of all primary teaching. Even with young children e-mails and
faxes can be used to exchange simple greetings and letters with children in
partner schools in other European countries where the language being
studied is spoken.

These activities illustrate the ways in which what primary teachers already
do can be applied to the teaching of primary MFL. In another part of the
curriculum emphasis is put on the issue of cultural awareness and here too
primary approaches fit in very well, given the primary teacher's traditional
concern with developing empathy and social understanding.

*To work with authentic materials, including newspapers, magazines, books, films, radio
and television, from the countries or communities of the target language.*
Primary teachers are very familiar with using these kinds of materials to
promote pupil learning. They are also very familiar with the idea of the
importance of creating a stimulating learning environment which reinforces
ongoing learning in the classroom. Primary teachers who take on the
teaching of a modern foreign language are able to recreate the atmosphere of
France, Germany, Spain or wherever the taught language is spoken by the
careful construction of displays, often using authentic materials gathered
sometimes themselves on trips abroad. And while in general the language
levels used in newspapers and other media productions are not likely to be
appropriate as teaching materials for direct primary modern language

teaching, there are all sorts of ways in which they can be used to promote language awareness and insights into the culture in which the language is embedded.

To come into contact with native speakers in the country where possible.
Again, the general point to be made here is that it is established good practice in primary education to involve 'real experiences' in pupils' learning, including encounters with 'real people'. Experts of all kinds are regularly invited into primary classrooms to add an element of authenticity to the learning taking place: real musicians, real artists, real community figures – police, fire, ambulance personnel, etc. And by the same token groups and classes of primary children regularly go out from school to meet such people in their real-life environments – concert halls, galleries, museums, hospitals, churches, etc. The value derived from these experiences depends crucially on the skills of the primary teacher in effectively exploiting the experience for educational purposes. Where primary teachers have been involved in primary modern languages they have often applied these skills to the use of native speakers, including foreign language assistants (FLAs) in the classroom, and also in planning rewarding trips to the country concerned. In the case of the Kent project referred to earlier, many schools have found it possible to visit France, even if only on the basis of a day-trip, and to organize an educational programme to support and promote primary MFL learning in exactly the same way in which they would promote say, historical and geographical understanding on a visit to Dover Castle or Canterbury Cathedral.

To consider their own culture and compare it with the cultures of the countries and communities where the target language is spoken.
The idea of ensuring that young children should develop a multicultural awareness has been an explicit feature of primary education for the past 25 years. Since the Swann Report of 1985, which made recommendations about preparing all children to live in a multiracial, multilingual and multicultural society, there has been overt official backing for the importance of familiarizing school pupils with a range of cultures other than their own. As suggested earlier, one of the main aims of teaching primary pupils a foreign language is to give the direct first-hand experience of 'living within' another language and culture so that they avoid the narrowness of monoculturalism and monolingualism. While it is the concern for promoting racial harmony and mutual understanding which has driven government policy on multicultural education, many of the practices primary teachers have developed to deliver a multicultural curriculum can nevertheless equally be applied to providing for this aspect of the MFL curriculum. In particular, the generalist role of the

primary teacher who is with the children all or most of the time enables him or her to mediate positive attitudes both implicitly and explicitly, through what is valued, celebrated and treated with care and concern. A primary teacher who with the class prepares an assembly for the whole school on the Hindu festival of Divali, and then effectively exploits the experience in a variety of follow-up activities and studies which include comparisons and contrasts with English religious festivals, could use exactly the same strategies to introduce Bastille day in France or mardi gras in Spain.

To identify with the experiences and perspectives of people in these countries and communities.
The kinds of active learning experiences referred to above, involving drama, role-play, simulations, artistic expression, craftwork, displays and so forth, specifically help children to identify with people from cultures with which they would not otherwise be familiar. Good primary teachers are engaged on this sort of venture across the curriculum. The development of empathy with others who are perceived as different is a key concern in much of the work primary teachers undertake in the area of religious education. Similarly, promoting children's understanding of how people felt, thought, worked and lived in earlier epochs and different countries underpins activities in primary history and geography.

To recognize cultural attitudes as expressed in language and learn the use of social conventions, eg forms of address.
At the primary stage children are still learning about the use of appropriate language in differing social situations in their own communities. Through work across the curriculum, but perhaps particularly in English and through literature, primary teachers draw children's attention to the ways that different circumstances require different linguistic registers and styles of vocabulary. They need to reflect, for instance, on the different ways in which they greet people, such as their friends as compared with the headteacher. In teaching a foreign language primary teachers can draw on exactly the same approaches, even in the early stages, for example in talking about the different situations in which in France one might use 'salut' or 'bonjour' as a greeting, and the fact that much greater use is made of 'monsieur', 'madame', 'mademoiselle' in addressing people. The overlap between the canons of good practice in MFL technology and the fundamental principles of primary education is clear.

Another aspect then of the MFL curriculum is the 'Areas of Experience'. These represent the curricular 'substance' or topics which should be taught. Five areas are identified, as shown below:

A. Everyday activities:

● the language of the classroom;
● home life and school;
● food, health and fitness.

B. Personal and social life:

● self, family and personal relationships;
● free time and social activities;
● holidays and special occasions.

C. The world around us:

● home town and local area;
● the natural and made environment;
● people, places and customs.

D. The world of work:

● further education and training;
● careers and employment;
● language and communication in the workplace.

E. The international world:

● tourism at home and abroad;
● life in other countries and communities;
● world events and issues.

Clearly there is a progressive outward movement from matters of immediate concern to young pupils towards the wider world of adult life. Sections D and E above are intended to be introduced only to pupils in KS4, ie after the age of 14. What is interesting about sections A, B and C, which are intended to be taught in KS3, ie to pupils between the ages of 11 and 14, is the extent to which they correspond with the primary curriculum in general. What is incorporated under 'everyday activities' corresponds with much which might be taught in primary schools in the areas of English – speaking, listening, reading and writing, science, physical education. 'Personal and social life' extends into areas covered in religious education and 'the world around us' opens out into geography, history and the arts.

In other words we are once again in terrain familiar to primary practitioners. We also return to the dilemma of the original NCMLWG, which, as noted above, did not like the idea that 'their' subject should be the only one to begin at KS3 rather than from the age of five like all others, though they felt at the time there was no other choice. What this meant, though, was that subject matter which could be seen as appropriate for children under 11 had to be taught to children over 11 because that was the point at which they were to start. At the time of their deliberations the TGAT report had established that there would be 10 levels of attainment to be defined for each subject. In the 1990 interim report by the MFL Working Group it is clear that there was again a concern that this subject should not be seen to be different from the others. It could be said that for a subject which starts 'half-way through' compulsory 5–16 schooling it might be appropriate to have less than 10 levels. The Group decided in the end that 10 levels should be defined so that MFL would not be different but also because at some point in the future foreign languages might be taught in the primary school. With this in mind they specifically described Levels 1–3 in ways which would provide suitable curricular material for teaching in the primary school. Throughout the subsequent changes in the National Curriculum this principle has been retained, and, as will be made clear in Chapter 4, most of the schemes in use in primary schools for the teaching of foreign languages comprise language structures and vocabulary taken from sections A, B and C above.

In what has been said in preceding paragraphs we have seen how what is nowadays 'officially' defined as how MFL should be taught draws heavily on what good teaching generally at primary level has long been about, and this point is developed further in Chapter 8. The argument throughout this discussion has been that because the principal features of effective MFL teaching and effective primary teaching now correspond so closely, primary teachers who are committed to the idea of introducing a foreign language into their primary teaching can do so by incorporating new subject matter (the appropriate structures and vocabulary of the target foreign language) into their existing range of pedagogical practices. This argument now needs further development by examining how the teaching of a modern foreign language can also be incorporated into the curricular content primary teachers have to deliver in the other subjects of the National Curriculum. In other words, having seen how the National Curriculum programmes of study for modern foreign languages which primary teachers do not have to teach actually prescribes things which they do teach, we can now look at examples of curriculum content which they do have to teach and see ways in which a foreign language could be taught at the same time. This idea of 'killing two birds with one stone', or 'd'une pierre deux coups', as the French say, is an important aspect of the principles of embedding and integration discussed in Chapter 1.

The National Curriculum is divided into core and other foundation subjects. The core subjects are English, mathematics and science; the other foundation subjects are design and technology, information technology, history, geography, art, music and physical education. Religious education is not actually a National Curriculum subject, although providing it is a statutory requirement imposed on all schools. Local Standing Committees on Religious Education (SACRE) made up of representatives from local faith communities draw up 'agreed syllabuses' for schools in their area. For each National Curriculum subject the programmes of study set out what pupils must be taught in each of the four Key Stages. In reviewing the content of these programmes for KS1 and KS2 it is clear that there are many opportunities for imaginative primary teachers to exploit the foreign language learning potential of what has to be taught across the primary curriculum.

MFL and learning across the National Curriculum

Cross curricular themes have undergone a series of different incarnations and conceptualizations over the past dozen years since the idea of a National Curriculum for England was first seriously mooted by politicians in power at the time. The new curriculum proposes a threefold classification:

● spiritual, moral, social and cultural development;
● key skills – communication, application of number, IT, working with others, improving own learning and performance, problem solving;
● 'other aspects of the curriculum' – thinking skills, financial capability, work-related learning.

These categories reflect the central policy concerns of the age, arguably in this instance the anxiety about moral behaviour and social control, skill acquisition to enhance employment prospects and then broader aspects of life as a responsible and independent citizen. This is demonstrated in the specific examples proposed.

In the case of spiritual, moral, social and cultural development the document simply gives one instance of the contribution of MFL for each adjective. Thus for spiritual education it is the role of provoking interest in meanings communicated through language and for moral education it is using the language to express opinions about right and wrong. These aims are really rather difficult to apply in the primary MFL context. On the other hand the emphasis in relation to social development on exploring customs and conventions and developing empathy and sympathy, and the value of MFL in pupils' cultural development through providing insights into difference in attitudes and behaviour, are directly relevant to long-established aims of primary education generally.

The concept of 'key skills' is assuming an ever higher profile in contemporary educational discussion as it becomes progressively more apparent that the traditional academic curriculum divided into discretely defined subjects does not constitute of itself a thorough preparation for the rigours of adult life in a rapidly changing technological society. MFL can clearly contribute to the developing child's awareness of communication, given that the whole enterprise is a communication activity, and the methods used, for example role-play and game activities, clearly also promote the capacity to work with others. Similarly, the whole communicative approach to teaching MFL described in other parts of the book encourages pupils to reflect constantly on their own performance and seek to improve. This aspect is discussed further in connection with the idea of 'graded objectives' presented in Chapter 9. Problem solving in MFL is harder to pin down, although in one sense the learning process itself is a problem-solving experience in which pupils have to make sense of alien sounds and words. And again, applying number is somewhat remote except in so far as numbers are generally taught in the early stages and can be applied in the context of currency, measures and distances.

IT, however, is a growth area par excellence. Good MFL teaching draws on IT resources and contributes to pupils' developing skills and understanding of information and communications technology. The Internet has made available to MFL teachers at all levels a wealth of language learning resources and direct access to native speakers in audio, visual and textual forms. It also allows for immediacy of communication across national frontiers using e-mail. In this way pupils can experience communication for real purposes with speakers/hearers/readers/writers of the target language. Many teachers also use faxes for the same purpose. Computers in general furnish a rich array of opportunities for progress-enhancing experiences through CD ROMs, audio and video conferencing, and downloaded programmes stored on hard disks, floppy discs, network facilities and Intranets. In particular, such programmes can give pupils simulated experiences enabling them to use the language in real social and cultural situations. The great advantage of much of this is that it permits pupils to work autonomously and independently and so control the pace of their own learning. It is a virtue of computers that they never lose patience and never become annoyed. Pupils can make the same mistake over and over again or fail to understand after *n* times of telling without there being any risk of the machine showing any irritation. Even the most calm, caring and tolerant teacher has limits beyond which it is difficult to avoid a slight 'edge' creeping into the voice. At the secondary stage, pupils who have difficulties with writing can be supported by using touch screens, adapted keyboards and the like, and this is also a good way to introduce and reinforce elementary writing with primary pupils. Computer-generated visual and sound displays from software programmes or the Internet can be used in direct teaching in a similar way to videos. For generalist primary MFL teachers this is of particular importance, given that there is a constant need for their pupils to be exposed to native speech models.

In considering its contribution to other aspects of the curriculum the National Curriculum document draws attention to the role of MFL teaching in encouraging thinking skills through putting pupils in situations where they have to figure out for themselves what unfamiliar language means, although this does seem very similar to the argument about problem solving. Familiarization with different currencies and exchange rates is suggested for financial capability. As to work-related learning, the document cites 'opportunities to cover work-related contexts within the topic of the world of work' but quite what this means in practice is left to the reader to deduce. Even at primary level some of this could be said to arise out of the material normally covered in the early stages, such as learning about places in town which are also of course part of the world of work.

Primary MFL and the core and foundation subjects

Just as teaching primary MFL enables pupils to progress in aspects of learning across the curriculum, so it also helps progress in some important elements of other curriculum subjects.

English is central to the whole curriculum and much of its curricular content relates directly to the teaching of primary MFL. With the advent of the literacy hour a substantial part of the English curriculum has been systematized in a programme of teaching based on a three-level framework, made up of word level, sentence level and text level. Many of the activities designated for each of these levels correspond to key activities in primary MFL teaching. Even though the emphasis in primary MFL is on oral work, this can have important consolidating implications for literacy as a whole. In the introduction to the National Literacy Strategy this point is clearly made: 'Good oral work enhances pupils' understanding of language in both oral and written forms and of the way language can be used to communicate.'

There are many specific ways in which primary MFL involves literacy-supportive experiences, in areas such as listening for different purposes, aural/oral discrimination and phonics, word and rhyme recognition, shared and guided listening and reading, reading at sight, using big books, reading familiar texts, memorization by heart, and etymological origins of vocabulary. However, to this list needs to be added the important effect, where it is well taught, of primary MFL on the child's whole attitude to literacy in general, including confidence to speak, listen and engage in communication. There is some evidence that this is especially important for boys and for children with special educational needs. Primary MFL can offer a 'fresh start' to pupils who have already experienced some degree of failure, and in this way can reinvigorate interest, motivation and commitment with positive experiences in French lessons spilling over into comparable activities in English lessons.

The statutory orders for mathematics are divided into four areas:

- using and applying mathematics;
- number;
- shape, space and measures;
- handling data.

Under the heading of using and applying mathematics particular emphasis is given to contextualizing mathematical issues in real-life practical contexts, and it is this which opens up possibilities for links with modern language learning. The examples of practical tasks involving mathematical processes used with pupils can be based on situations drawn from the country and culture of the language being taught. Some illustrative tasks in the case of French and France might be distances/journey times/costs of travel across France, transport timetables, currency changing calculations and commission rates, prices lists in cafés, restaurants and shops, etc. In the area of number multiples of ten and the decimal system can be studied using francs and centimes and metric measures. Actual numerical operations can be equally carried out using the French words for numbers, and primary children enjoy the novelty of reciting multiplication tables in French, helping them to remember, retain and recall. The statutory orders specifically refer to giving pupils opportunities 'to collect, record and interpret data from *an area of interest*, using an increasing range of charts, diagrams, tables and graphs'. All kinds of information about French life provide contextual references for such diagrammatic representation.

In the area of mathematics too the phenomenon of the 'fresh start' which primary MFL offers to pupils can have a revitalizing effect. Primary teachers have found that mathematical topics presented in French or another MFL can give pupils a 'second chance to learn' and instances have been reported of children learning to tell the time or learning tables in MFL lessons where they had not previously mastered these skills.

In the case of science and design and technology it is more a question of relating aspects of the programmes of study to French (or another) culture and civilisation. For example KS2 D and T section 5a 'investigating and evaluating a range of familiar products, thinking about how they work, how they are used and the views of the people who use them' could be applied to specifically French (or other products), for instance the place of coffee in French life and the machines which are used in the home and the café to prepare it. The spread of real coffee grinders and machines to English cafés is noteworthy in this regard in terms of rising demand for 'better' products. In the science programmes of study the section on living things in their environment could draw on studies of France, eg 5b 'identify similarities and differences between local environments and ways in which these affect animals and plants that are found there', where comparisons might be made between the local school environment and that of a partner school in France. Indeed, this cross-national comparison can provide the basis for all sorts of work in science, as the guidelines on Breadth of Study make clear: 'During the key stage pupils should be taught the knowledge, skills and understanding through a range of domestic and environmental contexts that are familiar and of interest to them.'

In facilitating the liaison between English pupils and their French (or other) partners ICT plays an increasingly important part, and in using it several different learning objectives can be achieved simultaneously. For example, in a project on 'life processes in the environment' (science) pupils can be involved in 'sharing and exchanging information in a variety of forms, including e-mail' (ICT) which requires them 'to develop and refine ideas by bringing together, organising and reorganising text, tables, images and sound as appropriate' (ICT and English) and the project might include aspects of designing, making and evaluating which contribute to the understanding of design and technology. The programmes of study for physical education make specific reference to the use of ICT in pupils videoing activity for the purposes of 'comparing ideas and quality' and 'to improve their performance'. It would be possible through the use of ICT facilities such as e-mail attachments, digital cameras, video conferencing and the Internet to involve partner schools in France and elsewhere in this process of physical expression and composition. The general value of ICT in MFL teaching was discussed above, and the corollary of this is of course that MFL lessons can be the vehicle through which a range of elements of the programmes of study for ICT can be delivered.

The three main languages taught in English schools come from countries deeply implicated in the historical development of Britain, and there are many opportunities to highlight France, Germany or Spain during lessons planned in accordance with the history programmes of study. In the post-2000 National Curriculum teachers are required to work on a European study which although focused on Ancient Greece is to examine the particular influence of belief, achievements and civilisation on the world today. The shared values of Western Europe can be taught through a study of key institutions and events in French (or other) history. The concept of 'citizen', for example, and its place in modern France and current debates in England could be usefully explored, taking in the French Revolution and the significance of ideas of liberty, equality and fraternity. In this way aspects of the Personal, Social and Health Education (PSHE) and citizenship programmes can be addressed at the same time, eg 4b 'to think about the lives of people living in other places and times, and people with different values and customs'. There is also here a significant contribution to the development of the European dimension in education, which is discussed in Chapter 5.

Links with France and other European countries are of manifest significance in the geography curriculum in relation to the provision of a contrastive case study of interest to pupils for many facets of the prescribed knowledge, skills and understanding, subdivided into 'geographical enquiry and skills, knowledge and understanding of places, knowledge and understanding of patterns and processes, knowledge and understanding of environmental change and sustainable development'. Under Breadth of Study instructions pupils are expected to 'study a range of places and environments in different parts of the world, including the United Kingdom and the European Union'. Europe is specifically designated as one of the three levels of 'locational knowledge' pupils should be taught. In this there is ample scope to combine geographical teaching with the teaching of a primary MFL. Similar types of knowledge linking the pupil's growing understanding of 'a foreign language in cultural context' with elements of National Curriculum orders can be identified in the case of art and music, where pupils should be taught about 'the roles and purposes of artists, craftspeople and designers working in different times and cultures', 'how time and place can influence the way music is created, performed and heard' and 'a range of live and recorded music from different times and cultures.' In the primary classroom there is scope for colourful and expansive displays of French geographical features alongside, for example, the art of the impressionists and the music of Debussy. Making the classroom a real learning environment has always been a noted strength of English primary practice and here par excellence is an opportunity to link together a range of subjects and educational objectives to achieve prescribed requirements through the medium of primary MFL.

In teaching all of the above subjects it is possible to incorporate the use of French language for real purposes through the use of straightforward general classroom instructions as well as the incorporation of discipline-specific vocabulary and phrases. An enthusiastic primary teacher of MFL, even without high levels of linguistic knowledge, can, for example, conduct much of a PE lesson using French words rather than English for key activities: 'Find a partner', 'Run', 'Jump', 'Hop', 'Stretch', 'Relax', 'Go!', 'Come here', 'Stop', 'Start', 'Play', etc. Given the commitment it really is not hard to learn a finite number of expressions which will then subsequently be repeated regularly as a normal feature of the regular teaching routine. The fundamental issue is persuading primary teachers during initial and in-service training that this an effort worth making.

National Curriculum rationale and primary MFL

A particular feature of the post-2000 National Curriculum is the amount of space devoted in its documentation to making explicit its underlying ratio-nale. Some of this is pitched at a very high level of abstraction, 'education should... reaffirm our commitment to the virtues of truth, justice, honesty, trust and a sense of duty'. Slightly more specific is the identification of two main aims of the 'school curriculum': the school curriculum should aim to provide opportunities for all pupils to learn and to achieve; the school curriculum should aim to promote pupils' spiritual, moral, social and cultural development and prepare all pupils for the opportunities, responsibilities and experiences of life.

Later four 'purposes' of the National Curriculum are itemized:

- to establish an entitlement;
- to establish standards;
- to promote continuity and coherence;
- to promote public understanding of the work of schools.

These are interesting value statements in the light of the primary MFL situa-tion. On the one hand, the Year 2000 National Curriculum proclaims univer-salism ('all pupils', 'entitlement', 'continuity and coherence', etc) and also links this with the provision of primary MFL: 'the learning of a foreign language in primary school provides a valuable educational, social and cultural experience for all pupils'.

Yet, on the other hand, the same curriculum does not require schools to teach primary MFL for reasons which are discussed throughout this book. It is no easy matter for any government to introduce a legal requirement on schools to teach something which the majority of them feel unable to deliver. It has therefore to be acknowledged that the present situation is an anomalous one. Quite how the tension arising from this anomaly might be relieved is a tricky question discussed in the final chapter of this book.

4

The primary curriculum

Levels of the primary school curriculum

The Year 2000 National Curriculum described in the previous chapter makes considerable use of the term 'the school curriculum'. The primary school curriculum is effectively divided into four levels:

- the National Curriculum;
- the basic curriculum – the National Curriculum + religious education (RE);
- the school curriculum – the basic curriculum + additional elements provided by the school;
- the whole curriculum – the overt school curriculum + the hidden curriculum.

These are all terms used in official documentation over the past decade, although the extent to which they have actually been absorbed into the everyday professional discourse of teachers and educationists is questionable. They are nevertheless a useful conceptual framework for situating the various constituent elements of the total curriculum offered to primary pupils.

The notion of the basic curriculum arises from the technicality that in England prior to the 1988 Education Reform Act, which introduced a National Curriculum for the first time, RE was in fact the only subject statutorily required to be taught. Previous legislation laid down the requirement that there be established local agreed syllabuses for RE under the supervision of the LEAs. Thus, although there was a national requirement to teach RE, the actual substantive content to be taught was determined locally. This position was left unchanged by the 1988 Act, and RE was never included as a national curriculum subject.

Schools are therefore in a situation where they are legally bound to provide the basic curriculum but are also called on to recognize that the basic curriculum is not the totality of the educational diet to be offered to their pupils. The amount of time between that which is legally required and the total time available is to be spent on school curricular content determined by the staff and governors of the school. For a number of years after the 1988 Education Act teachers, headteachers and other educational professionals complained bitterly about the 'overload' of the National Curriculum, and politicians and high-ranking officials in government departments and agencies vacillated over what percentage of the total time in school was to be spent on the National Curriculum and the basic curriculum. Then, in the mid-1990s, reforms prompted by an official review led by the Dearing Committee, reduced, as noted in Chapter 3, the extent of prescription and increased the amount of time left at the disposition of schools. This general principle has been left intact by the Year 2000 National Curriculum, although the earlier specification of an 80–20 split has not been made explicit in recent official documentation.

It is important though not to forget that the actual curriculum experienced by pupils does not just consist of the overt, intentional and explicit curriculum planned and delivered by teachers in formal lessons. Children learn a great deal from what has come to be called the hidden curriculum – that network of taken for granted assumptions, values, attitudes, beliefs, rituals and practices which comprise the school's distinctive ethos and culture.

In the previous chapter ways in which MFL can be articulated with the National Curriculum were explored. In this chapter issues surrounding the primary MFL curriculum itself that can be delivered as a discrete element of school curriculum time are considered, together with ways in which important messages about foreign languages can be communicated to pupils outside the context of formally taught lessons as part of the whole school culture.

Underpinning principles of the primary MFL curriculum

While one aim of this section is to suggest some indicative content for a programme of study for primary MFL, a more important concern is with identifying the principles underlying the selection and design of curriculum content. There are now a number of published schemes of primary MFL available and it is not the intention of this book simply to present another detailed sequence of material comprising another proposed scheme, although some indicative content will be suggested by way of illustration. Rather the hope is that the reader will be prompted to reflect on a series of key criteria against which published and other schemes might be judged. These include:

- the need to map out a series of topics which can be managed by generalist as well as specialist primary teachers;
- the need to ensure progression and continuity;
- the need for flexibility so that more confident teachers and more able pupils can go beyond basic structures;
- the need to contextualize the foreign language in situations which are accessible and meaningful to young children and which will arouse their enthusiasm;
- the need to achieve a sensible balance between providing enough vocabulary to facilitate short situated conversations and avoiding overburdening young learners or dampening motivation;
- the need to relate the form and content of the curriculum to the intended age range of pupils;
- the need to avoid introducing language content which carries unnecessary complication;
- the need to provide for reinforcement and effective learning of a defined, focused and circumscribed area of content;
- the need to be realistic about the likely time allocation for direct specific MFL teaching;
- the need to consider which language is to be taught.

As argued in other parts of this book, it is unlikely that the teaching of primary MFL on a widespread or universal scale can ever be operationalized with specialist teachers. There simply are not enough to cover both primary and secondary phases. As the Scottish national project has found, there will therefore have to be provision for MFL to be effectively taught by primary generalists. Any primary MFL curriculum, syllabus or scheme needs to have regard to this basic given of the situation. This makes providing for progression and continuity all the more important. Some subjects are arguably more linear and progressive than others. It might be said that in mathematics it is difficult to understand multiplication until there is some grasp of addition, or the subtraction of fractions until there is some grasp of the concept of equivalence. Other subjects, such as geography, may be inherently more modular in structure. It is though, of course, certain that there will be some mathematics teachers who will emphasize the modularity of mathematics and geographers who will maintain the linearity of their discipline. Nevertheless, in any subject it is probably easier to learn certain things if one has learnt certain other things beforehand. This is definitely true for foreign languages. The progression need not be purely linguistic, but can be also functional. Linguistic progression might be exemplified in the early stages by learning to count to 10 before learning the structure, 'I am x years old', or the numbers to 31 before learning the date. But there is also a functional element in, for example, learning to talk about having brothers and sisters after learning to explain what pets, if any, one has. In short there needs to be reflective thinking and explicit good reason for moving on to teach the 'next' bit of the language curriculum.

There is currently huge variation in the time allocated to direct specific teaching of primary MFL. If the subject is to emerge eventually as an integral part of the primary school curriculum it will be necessary to arrive at some consistency on this issue. It is likely that in the Scottish national project the total average time spent on the subject is less than one hour per week in practice. Most English primary teachers involved in MFL favour a 'little and often' approach. Much clearly depends on how ambitious the scheme to be taught is, and how it operates. In well-resourced schemes which provide for specialist input alongside the generalist class teacher it might be possible to arrange, say, 30–40 minutes each week with the specialist teacher, followed up with 10–15 minutes each day taught by the generalist class teacher. In fact it is probably not likely in present circumstances that even schemes based on generalists alone will be able to devote much more than 15 minutes per day.

Good primary MFL schemes need to evince their primary credentials and to be securely grounded in the ethos of primary education. They should not just be early-stage secondary textbooks relabelled for the primary market. As with any curriculum area, some published schemes are good and others are less good, and with the rapid growth of interest in primary MFL in England it is to be expected that the rate at which publishers produce new schemes will increase. The early languages Web site run by NACELL (at www.cilt.org.uk) displays details of many publications in the field, and proposals are in hand for the establishment of a system by which they can be evaluated by practising teachers of primary MFL whose judgements can then be accessed. There is also an intention to launch a 'kitemarking' scheme for new publications.

The primary MFL curriculum should be based on material which is relevant to pre-11 children. Scenes and conversations should be realistically set in places with which primary children can identify and in which they can imagine themselves actually being and acting, although this is not necessarily easy. To all intents and purposes now the primary age range runs from 3 to 11. Some nurseries are introducing foreign languages to their pupils. Commonly primary MFL projects focus on what used to be called the upper juniors: children aged 9–11. Schemes and syllabuses need to have regard not only to the age of the pupils being taught but also to the age span covered. Kent LEA's *Pilote* scheme, for example, is intended to provide a three unit programme to cover the three terms of Y6, the final year of primary schooling for children aged 10–11. Yet some 'all through' Kent primary schools have decided to break this down and 'spread it out' across all the infant and junior years. To make this work effectively much of the scheme has had to be redesigned to ensure both that it appeals to very young children and that there is reinforcement rather than repetition, and continuity rather than confusion over so many years of teaching.

Young learners need a crisply paced introduction of new content. Expecting them to assimilate large chunks of vocabulary is likely to be counterproductive in relation to both learning and motivation. Much better to focus on the key vocabulary necessary for sound and thorough acquisition of the language structure in question. In deciding on what vocabulary to include and what to exclude the primary MFL teacher should normally use the maxim 'when in doubt leave it out'. Primary pupils need enough words to enable them to engage in useful exchanges, and they should be given vocabulary which they want to use to express their own situation. Thus it was that the *Pilote* scheme came, as a result of so many of the county's children keen to speak about their beloved pet, to incorporate the French word for stick insect. It is *un phasme*, in case you did not know! This same principle applies in relation to the selection of language structures. In relation to asking directions, for example, it works perfectly well in France to say 'La gare, s'il vous plait'?, with a rising intonation to signal the interrogative. To try to teach the structure *pour aller à la (gare)* introduces the awful complexities of gender and number with, for example, *pour aller au (café)*, and *pour aller (aux magasins)*, all of which can be disastrous for primary teacher and primary pupil alike. Similar arguments can be advanced about introducing colours, which as adjectives have, in the formal jargon, to agree in kind and number and which follow rather than precede the noun in French. It depends of course. With able children, with a confident teacher, with intensive and sustained teaching, this may be absolutely appropriate. For the most part, however, so long as MFL remains an 'extra' which is not part of the defined and statutory National Curriculum, albeit mentioned in 'guidelines' in the sacred documentation, it is probably better to err on the side of caution.

It is the easiest thing in the world to make children dislike studying a foreign language. This is much more easily accomplished than the proverbial falling off a log. In the secondary school, MFL language learning is a compulsory part of the school curriculum and it serves no purpose whatever to send pupils on from the primary school with an already deeply entrenched dislike of French or whatever language had been attempted before age 11. It would be better to do nothing in the primary school than to arouse negative feelings at so young an age. This is why it seems preferable to concentrate on learning a focused and defined amount of the language with which both teacher and pupils can feel confident and comfortable, rather than trying to achieve unrealistic objectives which result in disappointment and disillusion on all sides. In the long run standards of achievement in MFL will be raised by successful teaching of MFL in the primary school. Superficially it may seem that setting excessively ambitious demands in the syllabus for primary MFL will 'raise' standards. In practice the reverse may actually occur if the demands simply cannot be met. Expectations need to be as high as they can be. If they are too low teachers and pupils will 'underperform', but if they are too high the same thing can happen because teachers and pupils either strive uselessly and frustratingly to get to grips with language which is way beyond them or they abandon the futile effort altogether. The way to raise standards is to do the most that can be done well and successfully.

While the indicative content suggested below is based on French for reasons given earlier, it could equally well be applied in the early teaching of other foreign languages. The issue of which language should be taught needs to be thought through very carefully by schools, LEAs and indeed responsible officials at government level. The injunction to 'diversify' is a long-standing *crie de coeur* of policy makers in the field of MFL teaching in schools. To a considerable extent it has been a cry in the wilderness in so far as it seems always to have come to little in the face of the massive inertia of the self-perpetuating system through which French teachers reproduce themselves from generation unto generation. Some take the view that the re-emergence of primary MFL risks making this regrettable situation even worse, because the most likely language that primary teachers will feel confident in teaching is French because they are products of the same French-dominated system of education. The arguments in favour of French are much less strong now than they were at the beginning of the century, when its hegemony began. It no longer rivals English as a world language. French hopes in this regard were finally dashed when English was officially adopted as the international language of air traffic control. Spanish and Portuguese are more widely spoken. German may be more important for business. Cantonese or Mandarin Chinese may be more significant in the later adult lives of children in primary schools at the turn of the millennium. And with the advent of instant communications and rapid transport the French are no longer quite so clearly the neighbours who we are most likely to meet 'abroad'. Every year after labouring through hard hours of learning French, youngsters board fast jet planes and fly right over France for the family holiday in Spain, Portugal, Italy or Greece. Given that what we are concerned with now is communicating it could be argued that it would be better to teach the languages of these countries.

This will nevertheless be 'a hard nut to crack'. A common argument advanced by teachers, primary and secondary, is that it does not matter which language is taught in the primary years because the child will have acquired language learning skills which can be applied with advantage to any new language begun at Y7, at the start of secondary schooling. This is probably true. Pupils and their parents, however, tend to be more hard-headed about the question. They tend to focus on the substantive content as well as the transferable skills. They regret the loss of all the words, phrases and expressions which are specific to French and which will not be built upon as children start again with German or Spanish or whatever. Such parental pressure can sometimes be deflected by convincing persuasion, but in the long run it has to be recognized that the effect of leaving primary MFL to local initiative is that it will become largely synonymous with primary French, and as a consequence diversification at secondary level will become more difficult to achieve. The answer in the end will be for 'the bull to be seized by the horns' at national level and to allocate resources to providing for diversification at primary level. This is discussed further in Chapter 7 in relation to teacher training.

Indicative content for the primary MFL curriculum

This section presents some indicative content of a possible MFL syllabus intended to cover Y5 and Y6. Although there is now great diversity in the extent of provision for pupils younger than 11, it remains commonly the case that schemes and projects designed to introduce MFL into primary schools are targeted at the nine-to-eleven age group, and the Year 2000 National Curriculum explicitly focuses on these two years in the KS2 range. In drawing up this syllabus the intention also has been to encourage teachers and pupils to 'bring France alive' in the primary classroom. Ideally this endeavour would be supported by the direct experience at some time during the two-year-programme of a visit to the country, even if it is only a day-trip to one of the port towns, complete with the bringing back on a massive scale of mementos, souvenirs, glossy leaflets, brochures and sundry realia to adorn both the classroom and individual project folders. This makes an immense difference to young children's perception of the reality of the language and usually provides for a huge boost in enthusiasm for further learning and exploration. However, even without this element, the skilled primary teacher can recreate an authentic French ambience in the classroom and assemble a positive context for the real situated use of the language.

For the purposes of structuring the proposed content in a systematic fashion the syllabus has been divided into six topics. These correspond roughly with the six terms of the two-year-period envisaged, but there may be good reason in particular cases for introducing material from later topics earlier, and of course there is always good reason for revisiting earlier topics later! In other words, this is not intended to be a hard and fast sequence.

Topic 1:	Teacher text:	Greetings and self-identification
	Pupil text:	Salut!
Topic 2:	Teacher text:	Exchanging personal and social information
	Pupil text:	Moi
Topic 3:	Teacher text:	In the café
	Pupil text:	Au café
Topic 4:	Teacher text:	Shopping
	Pupil text:	Le shopping
Topic 5:	Teacher text:	Finding the way around town
	Pupil text:	En ville
Topic 6:	Teacher text:	Living in France
	Pupil text:	En France

The proposed curriculum is intended to be operated in concertina fashion. It is really a basic indication of what it is reasonable to expect non-specialist primary teachers to be able, with some additional training support, to deliver to the pupils in their classes in the present circumstances. Some suggestions are given of where expansion may be considered, but these too are only illustrative. In this matter, as in all others, it is the professional judgement of the individual teacher in his or her particular circumstances that is most important in deciding whether to extend, and if so when, where and how.

The starting point for the teaching of any MFL, especially to young learners, is those aspects of language which are most directly related to the pupils' immediate personal experience. For this reason many primary MFL schemes have a first section devoted to greetings and personal details. In French there are good reasons to begin in the very first lesson with the one word, 'Bonjour!'. It is easy to learn and it can be practised enthusiastically in teacher–class, teacher–pupil, and pupil–pupil interaction. It should be accompanied by handshaking as happens in France. It does not need explanation, children will understand from the context that what is being done is greeting. It is definitely not necessary to suggest English translations. The teacher can simply seize a child's hand, shake it and say 'Bonjour, Mary!', encouraging the response, firstly by direct prompting, then by non-verbal exhorting 'Bonjour, Madame'. The teacher can lead the children, pied-piper style, one after the other, each greeting all the other pupils in turn around the class. In this way in a few minutes every child will have said and heard the word 30 times, and experienced 900 repetitions. The class could be split into teams to do the same thing in competition: child 1 at the front of the team greets each of the rest of the team in turn, then takes his or her place at the back; then child 2 does the same, and so forth until the last team member works his or her way from the front to the back. When this point is reached the entire team could chorus 'Bonjour' to signal completion. The teacher needs to engage in vigilant surveillance to ensure that everyone says the words properly and that there is no degeneration into unintelligible rapid mumbling! This kind of approach has the virtue of communicating to children that learning French is fun and that everyone can enjoy doing it. It also achieves the neat trick of dealing with a problem which all foreign language teaching has to solve. To learn a foreign language effectively you really have to be exposed to endless repetition, but repetition of itself is inherently boring. The trick is to find ways of producing repetition which is not actually experienced as repetitious and therefore boring, dull and demotivating. Game type activities, *activités ludiques*, as the French say, are a valuable way of resolving this particular conundrum. There are many *activités ludiques* which can provide a stimulating and exciting context for teaching language patterns, structures and vocabulary, even the one-word initial lesson on 'Bonjour'. Obviously the other greetings, 'Salut!' and 'Ca va?', can be presented and practised in exactly the same manner.

| Topic 1: | Teacher text: | Greetings and self-identification |
| | Pupil text: | Salut! |

Function	Language patterns/structure + key vocabulary
Greeting	Bonjour Monsieur, Madame, Mademoiselle Salut! Ca va? Ca va.

Taking leave of someone	Au revoir, à bientôt
Agreeing/disagreeing	Oui/Non
Thanking	Merci/Merci beaucoup/Merci bien
Asking/saying your name	Comment t'appelles-tu? /Je m'appelle…, et toi? Je m'appelle
Asking/saying where you live	Ou habites-tu?/J'habite à (town), et toi? J'habite a (town) dans le (county) en (country)

Once the pupils have been 'launched' in their language learning and can greet each other confidently and say who they are it is common to introduce them to questions and answers which will enable them to talk about themselves. The key structures are suggested below in Topic 2: Exchanging personal and social information.

Topic 2:   Teacher text: Exchanging personal and social information
            Pupil text: Moi

Function	Language patterns/structure + key vocabulary
Counting	Numbers 1–12
Asking/saying how you are	Quel age as-tu?/J'ai dix ans, et toi? J'ai dix/… ans
Counting	Numbers 13–31
Naming days	Days of the week
Naming months	Months of the year
Asking/saying when your birthday is	Quelle est la date de ton anniversaire? Mon anniversaire est le…, et toi? Mon anniversaire est le…
Asking/saying what the date is today	Quelle est la date aujourd'hui? Aujourd'hui c'est le…

Wishing someone happy birthday/ happy Christmas	Joyeux anniversaire/Joyeux Noël
Wishing someone happy saint's day	Bonne fête
Asking/saying if you have a pet	Tu as un animal? J'ai un chien/chat (+ additional pet vocabulary) Je n'ai pas d'animal
Asking/saying how many brothers/sisters you have	Tu as des frères ou des soeurs? J'ai deux soeurs, et toi? J'ai deux soeurs/je n'ai pas de frères

General principles of teaching these language structures and their associated vocabulary will be discussed in Chapter 8 but it is probably worth making one or two specific points at this stage. Pupils do need to appreciate the importance of tone of voice in asking questions, ie raising the tone at the end of the sentence. This is really a piece of language awareness, since it happens in English in much the same way. Direct questions can be asked by simply making the statement and lifting the voice at the end, 'Tu as un frère?' 'Tu t'appelles David?, etc. It is regularly practised in the greeting 'Ca va?', where the question and the answer are exactly the same, distinguished only by the rising intonation of the former. It is very useful to teach children the tag 'et toi?', because it is such a very simple way of formulating a question. The pupil quickly learns that all that is involved is stating what is true for him or herself and then adding 'et toi?' at the end. Pupils do though need to know the 'formal' styles of questions too because they are likely to be used in encounters with native French speakers. The sequence in which new linguistic items are presented is important because there are obviously some 'cumulative progressions', knowing the first 12 numbers before learning 'j'ai dix ans', for example. There is also here a gradual build-up of the number of vocabulary items which can be inserted into the language pattern being learnt. In the case of pets, this may require the teacher to consult a dictionary in order to ensure that every pupil is able to refer to his or her beloved hamster (*un cobaye*) or exotic fish (too many to list here!). More confident teachers with successful pupils may wish to add further structures to enable more to be said, for example:

Asking about/expressing what you like/do not like to do	Qu'est-ce que tu aimes faire? J'aime jouer au football Je n'aime pas dessiner
Strongly like/dislike	J'adore le football, l'histoire Je déteste la natation, les maths (+ additional sports/school subjects vocabulary)
Asking about/expressing preference	Tu préfères... ou... Je préfère...

The important point is not to jeopardize primary pupils' confidence. It is far better to do a little well than to attempt a lot and not really achieve any of it. Even without additional material, what pupils are able to say at the end of this topic still sounds quite impressive, eg

Bonjour, ça va? Aujourd'hui c'est le lundi douze mai. Je m'appelle Jane. J'ai dix ans. J'habite à Maidstone, dans le Kent en Angleterre. J'ai dix ans. Mon anniversaire est le dix-huit juin. J'ai une soeur, je n'ai pas de frères. J'ai un chien, deux chats et neuf poissons. Au revoir.

This kind of statement could be further elaborated by teaching *et* and *mais* so that the connective ands and buts give a more flowing natural quality to it. Nevertheless, as it stands it is something any pupil could be proud of being able to do in the early stages of learning French. Parents tend to be impressed as well!

There is a range of supplementary structures which able pupils might be able to manage in a group context. For example, using the third person form of the self-description/self-presentation structures: *Il/elle s'appelle, il/elle a dix ans, il/elle habite Dartford, il/elle a deux soeurs, il/elle a trois chats*, etc.

Once pupils are able to talk a little about themselves it is useful to be able to move them on into situations where they can interact directly in role play which could then be acted out for real on a visit to France. This can be achieved through the setting of eating and drinking in a café.

| Topic 3: | Teacher text | In the café |
| | Pupil text: | Au café |

Function	*Language patterns/structure + key vocabulary*
Asking for the menu	La carte, s'il vous plait
Asking for something from the menu	Vous desirez?/Qu'est-ce que vous desirez? Je voudrais... s'il vous plait (+ additional food and drink vocabulary)
Presenting	Voila/voici
Thanking	Merci/Merci bien/Merci beaucoup
Wishing someone an enjoyable meal	Bon appêtit
Understanding money	eg cinq francs dix centimes
Asking how much something costs	C'est combien? C'est... x francs... centimes
Asking about total cost	Ca fait combien? Ca fait... francs... centimes
Asking for the bill	L'addition, s'il vous plait Le service est compris?

The vocabulary for this topic is obviously made up of the various food and drinks on sale in cafés. This really is a topic which cries out to be contextualized in the primary classroom with a simulated French café in which pupils can act out the roles of waiter and customer. A large menu can be on display itemizing the price of *un croque monsieur, un sandwich au fromage, des frites*, etc. From this, students can move smoothly on to shopping.

| Topic 4: | Teacher text: | Shopping |
| | Pupil text: | Le shopping |

Function	*Language patterns/structure + key vocabulary*
Asking if items are available	Avez-vous un/une/des... s'il vous plait? Oui, j'ai un/une/des Je n'ai pas de Je n'en ai pas (+ primary shopping items vocabulary)
Asking for items	Donnez-moi... s'il vous plait
Understanding shop conversation	Et avec ça? C'est tout?
Asking how much something costs	Le/La/Un/Une..., c'est combien?
Higher levels of counting	Numbers to 100/1,000
Buying particular items: stamps ice creams bread and cakes	 Avez -vous des timbres pour l'Angleterre? Avez-vous des glaces? Quel parfum? (+ ice cream flavour vocabulary) Une baguette, des gâteaux
Understanding shop signs	Le tabac, la poste, la pharmacie, le marchand des glaces.

Shopping dialogues can follow broadly the same sequence as the café role-play. Previously learnt material can be brought in. The additional point is to be able to ask for something which is not on display or on a menu. The vocabulary items taught should cover objects which it is useful for pupils to know, either because they actually might want to buy these things on a trip to France, eg *une carte postale, des timbres (pour l'Angleterre)*, or because they are useful vocabulary items in the classroom, *un livre, un taille crayon, une gomme*, etc.

| Topic 5: | Teacher text: | Finding the way around town |
| | Pupil text: | En ville |

Function	Language patterns/structure + illustrative vocabulary
Excusing oneself to a stranger	Pardon Monsieur/Madame/Mademoiselle
Asking the way	La gare, s'il vous plait (+ additional places in town vocabulary)
Asking if something is near or far	La plage, c'est près/loin d'ici?
Giving /understanding directions	Allez tout droit Tournez à droite/à gauche Prenez la première, deuxième, troisième rue à droite/gauche En face de/ à côté de Devant/derrière
Asking what something is	Qu'est-ce que c'est?
Saying what something is	C'est un... /une...
Recognizing signs in town	SNCF PTT L'Office du Tourisme/ Syndicat d'Initiative Métro

Here too of course the focus is on structures and vocabulary which will be useful to pupils in practice during a visit. However, even without a visit, role-play and dramatization can occur in real-life simulations in the classroom or the school hall, where imaginary roads can be set up with signs and symbols to represent the places in town. Maps can be drawn or reproduced and used as the basis for explorations of where things are. A great deal is now available on the Internet and most major towns and cities have a Web site with a mass of useful information and potentially valuable teaching resources. It is often enough to type the name of a French city into a Web search engine to gain access to a wealth of material about the geography, history and customs of the place. Children also very much enjoy practising directions in 'human logo' contexts where a child is chosen to represent the screen turtle and then given directions in French in terms of a number of steps in a certain direction, eg 'allez tout droit – six, tournez a gauche – quatre, allez tout droit – deux, tournez à droite – cinq...', etc

---

Topic 6:	Teacher text: Pupil text:	Knowing about life in France En France
Function		*Language patterns/structure+ key vocabulary*
National symbols		Marianne (cf Britannia) La Tour Eiffel L'Arc de Triomphe Les Champs Elysées Nôtre Dame Le Tricolore L'Hexagone
Documentation		Carte d'Identité/Passeport
Les fêtes		Joyeux Nöel, pacques, Le quatorze juillet
Signs		Entre/Sortie Interdit WC/Toilettes
Asking the time		Quelle heure est-il?
Telling the time		Il est six heures Il est six heures et demie Il est six heures et quart/moins le quart Il est six heures vingt-cinq Il est sept heures moins dix Il est midi/Il est minuit

Asking about the weather	Quel temps fait-il?
Describing the weather	Il fait beau/mauvais
	Il fait du soleil/du brouillard
	Il pleut
	Il neige
The seasons	En été/hiver/automne
	Au printemps
Meals	Le petit déjeuner
	Le déjeuner
	Le diner
Saying in which country	En France, en Angleterre
Asking if someone speaks English/French	Vous parlez anglais?/Vous parlez français?
School timetable/language	L'emploi du temps
	Les matières – les mathematiques/
	le francais/l'histoire
	La recreation
	L'instituteur/Le professeur

It has to be emphasized that the items identified in the six topics above are, as suggested throughout, illustrative and indicative. Much more vocabulary would need to be included even with this intendedly constrained curriculum. It does not include either the language used in *embedding* (teacher commands, everyday routines, classroom objects, etc) or language to be used in *integration* across the curriculum. (These can be found in most published schemes.) It is certainly not prescriptive or exclusive. Other topics could be included, parts of the body, clothes, the extended family, etc, although it is always important to bear closely in mind what additional linguistic complexities each of these introduces for primary pupils and their teachers. What this indicative content is intended to do is to point to basic areas which motivated and trained primary generalists can manage well. In the absence of fully developed national programmes of study individual schools and LEAs will necessarily have to construct their own programmes in the light of their own circumstances, having regard to the 10 underpinning principles discussed earlier.

Similarly, the ways in which the syallabus might be operationalized, particularly in relation to the balance between the four language skills of speaking, listening, reading and writing, also needs to be carefully thought about in the context of the particular situations of given groups of pupils.

The QCA Scheme of work for primary MFL

In the Autumn of 2000 the QCA published a scheme of work for MFL at KS2, as described earlier. It is intended to provide 'a framework which will help schools to develop or adapt their own schemes. The materials are optional and meant to be used flexibly. Schools should feel free to use as little or as much of the scheme as they find helpful, adapting and selecting ideas as necessary to meet the needs of their children, to fit the time available and to meet the priorities of the school'.

This resource, which can be downloaded from the DfEE Standards Web site – at www.standards.dfee.gov.uk – is extremely useful. It provides valuable ideas and detailed guidance for teachers of primary MFL. The philosophy behind its design is pragmatic and realistic. Its authors say it is based on assumptions such as:

● Among primary schools that are teaching a foreign language there are many models, aims, objectives and teaching methodologies.
● There are considerable differences in the range and pattern of time allocated to learning a foreign language in different schools and areas.
● In some schools, teachers of the foreign language may have a high level of proficiency in using the language, but in other schools the subject knowledge of teachers may be limited.

It is possible to see the illustrative syllabus proposed above as one version of the QCA scheme based on a selection made for primary generalist teachers with limited prior knowledge of French. To deliver the whole QCA scheme of work would require a level of proficiency, and indeed a level of confidence, above that which many primary teachers might realistically be expected to have without further training. Nonetheless the presentation is accessible yet thorough and systematic. An enthusiastic primary generalist with a will to do so and good back-up resources could go quite a long way to mastering what is required to teach it. In each language it proposes 12 units:

1. I speak French/German/Spanish.
2. I introduce myself.
3. The family.

4. Pets.
5. My birthday.
6. The world.
7. Me and my school.
8. What would you like?
9. Sports.
10. Clothes.
11. Where I live.
12. A French speaking country.

There are some complications involved which non-specialists without training can find problematic, such as the agreement of adjectives, but teachers can simply avoid these items if they wish.

A particularly significant characteristic of this scheme of work is the extent to which it is based upon what is happening in primary schemes in use in local projects rather than on the secondary KS3 Programme of Study. This is an important development in 'official' thinking about MFL at primary level.

Planning the curriculum to raise standards

Raising standards of achievement in MFL means that at the point where progress is measured pupils need to perform increasingly well in relation to all areas assessed. Pupils need therefore to make progress in writing and reading the MFL as well as speaking it. However, because of the structure of the National Curriculum, with its defined attainment targets and levels, the impression can be gained that progress in the four attainment targets, speaking, listening, reading, writing, is expected to be parallel and uniform. In fact this is not necessarily so. Attention should be focused on the desired end result and thought given to the best way of achieving this. It could be that it would be better to give less emphasis to writing and reading in the early stages and a proportionately greater emphasis in the later stages. There are two main reasons for this.

Firstly, MFL teachers need to capitalize on the tremendous enthusiasm of all junior-age pupils for learning *to speak* a foreign language. Oral/aural learning in primary MFL is par excellence an inclusive subject. Children who have experienced academic failure in the rest of the primary curriculum, and children with all kinds of special needs, all have the chance to start something new at which all can succeed because it is focused on verbal human interactive communication. Once extensive formal writing and reading are introduced, the familiar spread of attainment re-emerges along with its sad accompanying stigmatization and self-identification of the successful and the failing, which then in turn leads to a spread of motivation. Children who might be capable of reaching good levels of attainment in speaking and listening can then fail to do so because of the demotivating effect of the subject becoming perceived as yet another area where they have difficulties with reading and writing.

Secondly, most of the school curriculum is devoted in one way or another to improving pupil's command of basic literacy. All academic subjects require a lot of reading and writing. The time available for MFL in either primary or secondary school is very limited, and MFL teachers have to consider very seriously whether they are using that time to best effect to promote pupil progress in the *target language as a whole*. In the later adolescent years pupils have much greater literacy skills all round and can use these to learn foreign language literacy much more quickly and efficiently than younger children. The sheer speed alone at which 15-year-olds can write compared with 10-year-olds ought to raise questions in our minds about whether it is a good use of time in a Y5 primary class to have pupils labour through foreign language writing which they would be able to do in seconds five years later. And ultimately, the end result may be that, when assessed, MFL standards in reading writing are higher, because in the early stages pupils acquired good levels of oral/aural understanding which were subsequently translated in to the written form rapidly and effectively once they had acquired the requisite generic literacy skills.

It is though very much a question of emphasis and balance. Nobody should be advocating that primary pupils do no reading or writing. Young children learning a foreign language need to see 'what it looks like' and to become familiar with the written form of words they would see around them in the country of the target language. These can be copy written, even by quite young children. Ideally the primary MFL school will have a partner school in the target language country through which pupils can be penpalled with each other, and they will want to exchange letters and other written papers, some of which should be in their respective foreign languages. As far as systematic teaching of reading and writing is concerned, however, caution should be the watchword. Time and time again I have encountered pupils whose spoken French and overall pronunciation was good until they saw the spelling of the words. *Deux* then becomes *deuhcks*, *le pain* becomes *lee pane*, and so the depressing litany of unlearning proceeds. This is of course not inevitable, and sensitive teaching can overcome it. French may be more problematic in this respect than either Spanish or German. It is helpful to point out to pupils learning French that where words end in *s*, *t* or *x* the final letter is not sounded. Nevertheless it has to be acknowledged that teaching the written form of the language at the primary stage does constitute an added difficulty for both pupils and teachers, especially the primary generalist class teacher. There are four important principles to bear in mind.

- The written form should only be introduced when the oral form is secure; pupils should read and write what they already understand and know how to say.
- Extended writing should generally be avoided.
- The relationship between oral pronunciation and written spelling should be discussed (as in the above example of French spelling).
- Reading and writing the MFL provides opportunities to raise pupils' language awareness which should be exploited, eg common roots with English words and phrases, but this should not lead to complicated expositions of grammar.

An advantage of teaching pupils the written form of the MFL utterances they are familiar with is that they can actually see where one word ends and the next word begins. This too is perhaps a more difficult issue in French than in other languages. It is not uncommon to see primary pupils, especially the more able, actually trying to write down phonetically the foreign language sentences they know. This is a clear indication to the teacher that they are ready for the written word. It is also an indication of the extent to which they are using writing as part of their overall learning strategy in any area, and it would be ridiculous not to build on this highly desirable development. Over the years MFL teaching has been an area where constricting orthodoxies have sometimes prevailed. Maybe now what is called for is a degree of pragmatism. 'No written word' or 'writing right from the first lesson' are extremes to be avoided. Especially in the present situation, where primary MFL is non-statutory and based on local initiative, teachers need not simply follow the prescribed orthodoxy but should be sensitive to what works and what does not work and why.

Exactly the same considerations apply to 'grammar'. With systematic teaching over an extended period, even if it is exclusively oral, primary pupils will begin to wonder why things are said in the way they are, and it is reasonable that they should be given some explanation. An obvious example is gender. In classroom vocabulary children are likely at some point to think it odd that they have to ask for *une gomme* but *un crayon*. It is enough to point out that in French there are two groups of words/nouns, a group of *une* words and a group of *un* words. In English we have only one group of nouns. The link could be made between *un* and *le* and *une* and *la*. It is not necessary to go into the issues of masculinity and femininity, although with some groups of pupils it may be appropriate. On the whole it is important not to make a fetish of grammar, and we do well to pay heed to the advice given by John Locke more than 300 years ago: 'French should be talked into the child... Grammar is only for those who have the language already.' (quoted in Hawkins, 1999.)

Overall thus what to teach in primary MFL remains for the time being very much a question of planning with local circumstances in mind. There will always be limited time and the curriculum needs to be geared towards making most effective use of that time to raise standards. Standards are not, however, only to do with formally tested linguistic knowledge and skill. Standards are also to do with attitudes and behaviour, and crucially attitudes towards 'foreigners', particularly fellow members of the EU. MFL has an important contribution to make to the European dimension in education, and this is examined in the next chapter.

5

Primary MFL and the European dimension

What is the European dimension?

The 'European dimension in education' is essentially about preparing children living in the member states of the EU for their future lives as adults within an increasingly interdependent continent. Time was when to argue that schools should teach pupils about 'being European' would have been regarded as propagandizing from a partisan standpoint. There have always been and of course continue to be 'pro Europeans' and 'Eurosceptics', but as regards the place of teaching about Europe in schools the situation changed formally in 1988 when the famous 'Resolution of the Council and the Ministers of Education meeting within the Council on the European dimension in education' was passed and signed, incidentally, on Britain's behalf by the unlikely figure of Kenneth Baker, then Secretary of State for Education. From this point onwards the view that children should be prepared for life as European adults became official government policy. The resolution 'launched a series of concerted measures' and all the member governments were supposed to take steps to implement them immediately within their respective systems of education. Specifically the measures aimed to:

- 'strengthen in young people a sense of European identity and make clear to them the value of European civilisation and of the foundations on which the European peoples intend to base their development today, that is in particular the safeguarding of the principles of democracy, social justice and respect for human rights';
- 'prepare young people to take part in the economic and social development of the European Community and in making concrete progress towards European Union, as stipulated in the European Single Act';

- 'make them aware of the advantages which the Community represents, but also of the challenge it involves, in opening up an enlarged economic and social area to them';
- 'improve their knowledge of the Community and its Member States in their historical, cultural, economic and social aspects and bring home to them the significance of the co-operation of the Member States of the European Community with other countries of Europe and the world'.

The Resolution also identified some specific actions to be taken. It was felt that governments should produce written policies to be set out in clear documentation which could be sent to all schools, and that this should feed into the ordinary processes of curriculum planning. The policies developed should embrace all disciplines, and curriculum statements and teaching materials should make explicit how the European dimension is being addressed, especially in the areas of literature, modern languages, history, geography, social sciences, economics and the arts. In the same way the resolution proposed that the European dimension should be explicitly included in initial and in-service teacher education and training. In conjunction with these actions governments were also urged to establish measures to boost contacts between pupils and teachers from different European countries.

The extent to which any of this actually happened in the sense of becoming lived realities for teachers and pupils in the following three years is rather a moot point. Nevertheless, in February 1991 the British Government published a statement of its policy and a report on activities undertaken to implement the Resolution. The policy itemized a number of key elements it saw as crucial:

- helping pupils and students to acquire a view of Europe as a multicultural, multilingual community which includes the UK;
- encouraging awareness of the variety of European histories, geographies and cultures;
- preparing young people to take part in the economic and social development of Europe and making them aware of the opportunities and challenges that arise;
- imparting knowledge of political, economic and social developments, past, present and future, including knowledge about the origins, workings and role of the EC;
- promoting a sense of European identity, through first-hand experience of other countries where appropriate;
- promoting and understanding of the EC's interdependence with the rest of Europe and with the rest of the world;

- encouraging an interest in and improving competence in other European languages.

While it is of course the last point which concerns us most directly here, it is also important to bear in mind the ways in which good teaching of MFL in both primary and secondary schools can contribute to pupils' development in relation to all of these areas. Nevertheless, a decade later it is sobering to reflect on the extent to which these are still ideals to be striven towards rather than objectives clearly achieved.

The European dimension and MFL teaching

In 1992 the Department for Education and Science published *Policy Models: A Guide to Developing and Implementing European Dimension Policies in LEAs, Schools and Colleges*. This document actually only devoted a single page to examples of specific activities and projects undertaken in England and Wales to promote the European dimension in education. It does not refer at all to the learning of MFL in primary schools. It does though clearly emphasize the central importance of MFL teaching in secondary schools, highlighting the opportunities the subject offers for pupils to: 'consider and discuss the similarities and differences between their own culture and those of the countries and communities where the target language is spoken... and become increasingly aware of cultural attitudes expressed in language' (DES, 1992: 15).

The document appears to take for granted the assumption, which is probably widespread, that to teach a modern foreign language is itself to provide a 'European dimension' in the curriculum. It is not uncommon in secondary schools to find that any communication to do with the European dimension, eg copies of the bulletins regularly sent out by the United Kingdom Centre for European Education, are automatically forwarded to the Head of Modern Languages. This kind of thinking, however, misses the central point of the European dimension. To pigeon-hole it as just something for MFL teachers to think about and respond to is to misunderstand the intention of transforming the whole of pupils' experience in order to prepare them for a different kind of Europe than the one inhabited by their parents' and grandparents' generations. To send the message that no other part of the curriculum needs to be concerned with it is indeed to diminish it. Even to send the message that it is only part of the formal taught curriculum, and not part of the wider school environment and community, is also to diminish it.

There is of course no guarantee that even the partial provision of a European dimension in children's experience through MFL teaching will necessarily be positive. Depending on how the languages are taught, it is perfectly possible for children to sit through lessons in French, German or Spanish without having any of the stereotypical preconceptions they may have acquired from their home culture about the inhabitants of France, Germany or Spain being seriously challenged, or worse still, actually having them confirmed. In fact they may discover that the French do eat snails and frogs' legs, Germans do have strong rules which must be obeyed, Spaniards do carve up bulls alive and in public, without simultaneously acquiring the cultural insight, sensitivity and empathy which would enable them to put these realities in a meaningful human context with which they can identify and sympathize, and so understand. The result of this lack can be that they simply take the literal confirmation of the gross stereotype as proof that all the negative images are true, generalize to the whole society, and never get beyond this. To arrive at this dismal point is not only to fail to deliver the European dimension, and probably to fail to teach the language since motivation to learn the language of negatively valued people is likely to be weak in the extreme, it is also the antithesis of education which, if it means nothing else, must surely be about opening minds up rather than narrowing them down. Language teaching well done can certainly reverse this scenario, by presenting a positive image of the language and the culture within which it is embedded, and by developing an openness of mind in which cultural diversity is positively valued. However, this task is greatly facilitated where there is a real commitment to incorporating the European dimension in both the overt and the hidden curriculum of the school. And once again, it can be argued that primary schools are better placed to do this than are secondary schools. The primary generalist teacher who is responsible for all or most of the taught curriculum can ensure much more easily that the same 'messages' come through the various subjects than can the staff of a secondary school where complex processes of inter-departmental collaboration are necessary.

As far as language teaching per se is concerned the crux of the matter is developing the pupil's appreciation of the interrelationship between language and culture. The contribution of the language teacher to the European dimension is to help pupils to realize that people living in other member states of the EU are both the same and different in relation to their language and the way they live, and that they are to be valued for both their sameness and their difference. They are the same in terms of the human universals which underpin all linguistic and cultural systems and they share common features of a European cultural heritage. On this basis we can identify with each other and share a sense of belonging. They are different in terms of the cultural and linguistic particulars, the food they eat, the sport they enjoy, and the way they conjugate verbs or construct sentences, but these differences are to be seen as enrichments to be enjoyed and celebrated rather than alien threats to be feared and disliked. Pupils need to learn that it is fun to talk in another language, to eat different kinds of food, to try different cultural experiences. Mediating these kinds of attitudes is an integral element of the role of the modern foreign language teacher. It is in these sorts of ways that any teacher of foreign languages can contribute to the development of the European dimension in schooling. In considering specifically what the role of the *primary* MFL teacher might be in relation to delivering the European dimension it is perhaps useful to break the issue down into the following six elements:

● European identity;
● European life cycles;
● increasing mobility in Europe;
● the European cultural heritage;
● the idea of Europe;
● teaching about Europe.

Primary MFL teaching and European identity

The various selves which make up the integrated personality of each individual can be usefully conceived of as a set of superimposed concentric circles. At the hub, the innermost circle, is the identity arising out of the individual's relationships with family and friends. Beyond that is the individual's identification with the particular village or town in which they live, or from which they originate, and then the region to which they feel they belong and finally their national identity as a citizen of a particular country.

Put like this the idea seems simple and straightforward; in practice of course the difficulties involved in this superimposition are immense. European adults have shown themselves ready to die for their country; it is questionable how many, even amongst the ranks of the 'Euro-enthusiasts' would be prepared to die for 'Europe'. During the Wars of the Roses people born in what is now Lancashire and Yorkshire were willing to die for their respective regions. The gradual superimposition of an English national consciousness has now made this obviously unthinkable, however much residual mutual suspicion still lingers either side of the Pennines. The proposition is that the same basic process now needs to operate at the European level so that formerly separate and often hostile nations can share a common broad identity. This process, however, is impeded by the centuries old antagonisms and mutually negative stereotyping which the various nations of Europe have developed towards each other.

In the case of England and France such reciprocal denigration has always provided a rich vein for humorists of all kinds to mine. When the Channel Tunnel project was first announced a cartoon appeared in a French newspaper showing a map of the British Isles with an arrow emerging from Folkestone, circling round the Kent peninsular and leading into the North Kent coast. The map was labelled: 'Channel Tunnel: The English Plan'. In another famous cartoon a stereotyped Frenchman, complete with baguette and beret, berates a stereotyped Englishman carrying an umbrella, with a long list of all the iniquities visited by the English on the French from the Hundred Years War onward. With evident disdain the only response considered necessary to this tirade is 'frog's legs'. Nothing more needs to be said about a nation capable of such an abomination! Another neat Anglo–French encounter encapsulated in cartoon form is the drawing of two soccer yobs, complete with Union Jacks, England scarves and rosettes, in front of the Bayeux tapestry and commenting: 'You see, it was the French who were the first to send over the hooligans!'

There can be no doubt that hostile stereotypes are antithetical to the development of a harmonious Europe. There is evidence that they are acquired very early in life, and it is this which makes the provision of a European dimension in primary schooling so important. Research undertaken by Bell (1989) on the teaching of Europe in the primary school concluded that: 'Pupils do not normally see themselves as Europeans or recognise much relevance of Europe to their lives... Pupils' opinions and beliefs about Europe are often simple and distorted, but nonetheless often firmly formed and expressed.'

Similarly, in researching the attitudes of children in the final year of primary schooling in the North of England, Escarte-Sarries found in 1990 that: 'The types of images of France and French culture which pupils had before starting French in secondary school are therefore often inaccurate and stereotyped.' She recommended that teachers should tackle directly the distorted images contained in stereotypes so that: 'By giving them a framework with which to help them interpret their impressions pupils might be enabled to go beyond viewing everything from a British norm.'

Whether or not much attention was paid to pupils' understanding of their European citizenship used, at least in England, to be a question of political, personal and professional opinion. With the 1988 Council of Ministers Resolution, the 1992 DES guidelines, and the implications of the Maastricht treaty, it is now official policy.

The introduction of MFL teaching in the primary school can assist youngsters directly to experience 'Europeanness' through the ways in which the teacher 'brings alive' things French, German or whatever in the classroom. Provided the primary teacher of MFL succeeds in integrating the foreign language into the classroom in the ways suggested in this book, the children will see the language rather than the foreignness, will begin to identify themselves as the kind of people who are 'naturally' multilingual and multicultural, and will define themselves as sharing rather than opposing the language and culture being taught. In this way they can be initiated into the concept of a Europe as community of which they are a part. The primary years have always been the time in which children learn to feel they belong to wider communities beyond the immediate intimate circle with whom they interact on a face-to-face basis, notably the period during which they acquire the foundations of regional and national identity. Through carefully planned positive experiences of the language and culture of another member state of the EU in the way suggested elsewhere in this book they can come to appreciate that the boundaries of the human community with which they strongly identify go beyond their national borders.

Primary MFL teaching and European life cycles

We tend to talk about the life cycle and view the process of birth and death as somehow part of an ongoing circular evolution through the seven Shakespearean ages of man from 'mewling infant' through to the alarmingly similar final stage of being 'sans hair, sans teeth, sans everything'. What is incontestable is that in the late 20th century European developments profoundly changed some of the key factors which influence how the life cycle is lived out. European legislation now affects every aspect of life from the cradle to the grave. Decisions taken within the Commission, the European Parliament and the Council of Ministers impact directly on the everyday lives of people in Calais, Canterbury, Cologne, Calabria, Catalonia and Copenhagen, even if for the moment most of them do not think much about it or fully realize it. It is actually no longer sufficient for French citizens to think only as far as Paris to the Assemblée Nationale, l'Elysée and the Hotel Matignon, any more than the thoughts of the subjects of Her Majesty should extend only to London, Downing Street and the Houses of Parliament. We are now all affected by European levels of government, from infancy (eg maternity/paternity rights) to old age (eg regulations governing pensions).

Furthermore, since 1 January 1993 and the advent of the Single Market, children leaving school and students leaving university no longer go into a national labour market but now find themselves in a huge job market of 350 million. Here they enter into competition with job-seekers from all over Europe, not only on grounds of technical skill, competence and qualifications but also in relation to the appropriateness of their attitudes and their linguistic skill. Many job advertisements now specify that applicants should have the ability to speak another, sometimes two other, European languages. More significant from the point of view of the European dimension in education is the increasing number of references to internationalist attitudes. In a recent edition of the French newspaper *Le Monde*, the following specifications for applicants were far from untypical:

'À l'aise dans un milieu international, vous parlez très bien l'anglais.' ('At ease in an international milieu, you speak very good English.')

'Votre pratique courante et impérative de l'anglais et de l'allemand vous a donné une culture et des convictions européennes.' ('Your required fluency in English and German has given you a European culture and European convictions.')

These are important realities of the adult world for which we need to prepare our pupils. In a real sense pupils who do not have the requisite attitudes will be seriously disadvantaged. It has always been the responsibility of schools to ensure that pupils have a basic understanding of their future role as citizens. The issue is, though, citizens of what? What happened at the end of the 20th century was that the context of that citizenship widened. Whether or not it is widely appreciated, the formal position is now that most people living in Western Europe are legally citizens of the EU, as well as of one of its constituent nation states. Their common passports make this absolutely clear. The framework of political, judicial and legal structures in which citizenship is nested is significantly European. To allow young children to grow up now without thinking of themselves as at least partially European is arguably to fail to educate them. It remains to be seen whether the recent introduction of citizenship education as a formal part of the National Curriculum will really impact on children's identity in this way.

The primary school teacher of MFL, especially the generalist teacher who is in a position to reinforce the same points throughout the curriculum, is well placed to help children to understand the extent to which their lives are affected by European issues. In lessons on the language of shopping, for example to practise structures such as *je voudrais… (une pomme, un café, une glace*, etc), teachers can discuss with pupils the 'Europeanness' of products on sale, their country of origin, and the ways in which they are subject to European conventions and regulations. They can talk about products which were distinctively, say, French, but which we now routinely buy in England, such as croissants or baguettes. They can intervene in pupils' thinking on wider matters, helping them, for example, to get beyond the superficial, xeno-phobic tabloid derision aimed at 'straight banana' type rules to consider the rationale behind Europe-wide agreements, regulations and specifications which are intended to benefit producers and consumers in all parts of the

Union. A generalist primary teacher of MFL might be able to take the issue further in, say, English lessons and compare the different stances taken, and the varying styles of text used, by different newspaper reports on topics in this area. In this way pupils' awareness of how Europe does and should impinge on their lives can be developed, alongside a dawning realization of the extent to which attitudes towards Europe in general and other countries in Europe in particular are deeply ingrained in the home culture of the country in which they are growing up.

Primary MFL teaching and increasing mobility in Europe

Mobility in the modern world has increased dramatically in every sense and this is having profound implications for how European children should be educated.

The speed and efficiency of travel has drastically reduced journey times such that distances which used to require days now take only hours or even minutes to cover. The Channel Tunnel now enables an overall journey time of three hours between London and Paris, and 25 minutes between Folkestone and Calais. In a real sense this brings the countries of Europe closer together. The time distances between countries of the EU are what were formerly the time distances between regions within a single country. This 'closeness' means that it is no longer reasonable to regard other parts of Europe as being, in Neville Chamberlain's memorable phrase, 'faraway countries of which we know little'. We have to recognize the implications of our proximity in all senses to other European nations.

Nowadays there are simply more people moving about across national borders, for reasons connected with holidays, work, family and friends. As a consequence people are exposed to a much greater range of cultural variation than was generally the case previously, and accordingly they are likely to develop more cosmopolitan views and greater open-mindedness. In general, populations in any given area of the EU will become more diverse and less stable over time. Children directly experiencing family mobility tend to have a particularly strong natural adaptability, and this is a resource teachers practising the European dimension in education should surely exploit. Legion are the stories of multinational children on Europe's beaches establishing friendships in the face of what adults tend to regard as insuperable language barriers. During a recent research project in France the author encountered an English child by the name of Riley who had moved with his family to Calais and become a pupil at a primary school included in the study. Calling the register French teachers invariably gallicized the pronunciation of this name, 'Reeley'. With his then very rudimentary grasp of the language of Molière, the indignant child would protest, 'Non, je m'appelle *Riley!*' By the end of the year the teachers had made some progress, and could manage a passable 'Riley', but by then the boy had moved on too, had got a grip on nasal '*n*'s, rolling '*r*'s and the intricacies of conjugations, and no longer wanted to be marked out as different from his French peers. He still protested, but now in faultless French, that his name should be pronounced 'Reeley'.

Even if people do not physically travel around they are likely to be involved in much more 'mental travelling', in more communications with more people from more countries. In the run-up to the coming into force of the Single European Act in 1992 Clive Saville, who was Head of Teacher Supply and Training at the DES, in a speech to the European Association of Teachers in 1989, observed that:

> It doesn't just mean that more people will move around Europe looking for jobs in the manner of *Auf Wiedersehen, Pet*, but that for far more people work will become more European in some way whether they move or stay at home. Many more jobs will have an international dimension; more people will travel as part of their jobs, even if they are not based abroad; at the most mundane level people will have to get used to taking telephone calls in another European language; more often the competition for a particular contract will come from another European country; more firms will be international in their management struc- ture, their manufacturing or operating base and the destination of their products or services. If we use the shorthand 'mobility' to cover all of that then... we must prepare our young people for 'mobility'.

Since this statement was made, over 10 years ago, there has of course been a massive expansion in this wide sense of mobility. Huge developments have taken place in ICT. The World Wide Web, the information superhighway and e-mail have brought the possibility of instant communication with anyone, anywhere at any time. Languages and cultures are thrown into a kind of 'cyberspace melting pot' where people can interact and exchange across social, political, national and international boundaries. The primary teacher of MFL can mobilize these different sorts of mobility simultaneously to promote children's learning of the foreign language and to prepare them for the high- speed, high-tech European environment they will inhabit in their adult lives. Many teachers will want to organize actual mobility for their pupils in the sense of travelling to France or wherever. Others will prefer to make contact with French teachers and pupils through linking up with 'partner schools' and exchanging letters and other artefacts and documents either through the post or through electronic media. The important point to make here is that if we do not prepare pupils for this world of social, geographical and 'psychological' mobility and rapid communications we are not really fulfilling the role of educators.

Primary MFL teaching and the European cultural heritage

It could be said that a major role of the European dimension in education is to foster pupils' understanding of the extent to which the national cultural heritage that is so pervasive in their everyday lives is actually part of a wider European cultural heritage.

This common European heritage is manifest at several levels of experience. At the highest levels it is the European culture which produced and dissemi-nated important human values such as democracy, justice and freedom. In cultural fields such as music, art and literature the movements and the great names are European. Beethoven, Brahms and Bach may all have been German but their musical genius is European in nature. Dante, Göethe and Shakespeare all share a common European universe of literary discourse. At the level of popular culture many folk tales have been shared down the centuries across the continent, and with the global village brought into being by the media of mass communications the commonality of experience of everyday life has developed apace.

Teaching children how truly European their national culture is should not be seen, as is sometimes suggested, as a threat to their national identity, but rather as an enrichment. Lejeune (1978) argues that: 'It is vital for us to become familiar with our roots in order to understand that we Europeans are but the branches nourished by the ancient sap of a single tree. The branches differ, the trunk is the same; the countries differ, their origin is the same. This diversity in unity is what makes up Europe.'

The idea of presenting children with 'diversity in unity' is pretty much what teaching modern foreign languages is really about. It is about seeing the commonalities and the differences, but noticing that even in the apparent differences there are common themes. The names of the days of the week, for example, look and sound different in English, French and German but there are common ideas behind them. 'Once upon a time' and *il était une fois* are different phrases which both invite European children into the same imagi-nary land of wonders and marvels. In discussing *centimes* in lessons involving French money, English children can be encouraged to reflect on just how common in both languages is the use of 'cent' to indicate one hundred. Pointing out the extent to which English 'national' culture and language are actually European is not to diminish the value of national identity but rather to tell the truth about it. From a narrow nationalistic standpoint much 'national culture' is actually imported from other countries. But the 'importation' of great music or art is not actually experienced as such, even by 'nationalists', precisely because of the extent to which we all already share European tastes, sensitivities and forms of understanding. Whatever else education is, it is surely about telling children the truth!

Primary MFL teaching and the idea of Europe

In the last decade the world has shifted from bi-polarity in the era of the Cold War to the current situation of 'multi-polarity. In the new world power game Europe as whole is a major player. As small individual nation states European countries cannot achieve as much independently as they can by working cooperatively. The world is increasingly made up of regional power blocks in which there is much less room for separate nation states. People from other parts of the world tend only to see 'Europe'; Americans are much more likely to talk of going to 'Europe' than to list the individual countries their trip is going to 'take in'. In certain world councils there is only representation from the EU as a whole, not from individual European countries. There are certain problems that can only be solved at a Europe-wide level, pollution and the protection of the environment for example.

This idea of the wholeness of Europe is experienced as strange by many whose identity is filled with national commitment. Yet, historically speaking, these nation states which people are so proud to belong to are comparatively recent inventions. There was a time when, at gatherings of the inhabitants of what are now France, Spain or England, for example, those present might all have been addressed as *cives romani*, and then in the time of Charlemagne and on into medieval Christendom and the Renaissance there was always an awareness of the continent as a whole entity with considerable mobility and few restrictions. The careers of bishops of the church, for instance, often embraced appointments across the continent. It was not at all uncommon for them to hold positions in what are now clearly different nation states. In this sense Europe was united for longer than it has been divided.

We are now in an era where we and subsequent generations need to recover the idea of Europe's wholeness. Children need to understand that Europe has been a social, cultural and political whole in the past and that it is regaining its wholeness in their lifetimes. The programmes of study for history in the National Curriculum require primary pupils to become familiar with various periods of European history. Something of this will surely continue even now that there is no longer a statutory obligation on schools to follow the programmes of study. The primary MFL teacher can set this in context by enabling children to appreciate why there is such a desire on the part of many in Europe now to heal the disastrous divisions of the past, and the role that learning one another's languages can play in bringing this about.

Primary MFL teaching and teaching about Europe

The European dimension in education needs to be an ongoing part of children's whole school experience if the aims of the 1988 Declaration and those set out in the subsequent official documents referred to above are to be achieved. It should merge into all elements of schooling: into the disciplines of the formal curriculum and into the attitudes, values and beliefs transmitted through the hidden curriculum. The European dimension is a cross-curricular theme which should *permeate* the entire curriculum.

There is a distinction between teaching about Europe and providing a European dimension in education. Much of the teaching about Europe is done within traditional disciplines such as history, geography, music and art: providing children with basic facts and knowledge about Europe. Providing a European dimension in education, however, has much more to do with skills and attitudes. Indeed, it is arguable that this aspect of education, attitudes and skills, has assumed much greater importance in education in the modern world, generally. Facts and knowledge are easily forgotten and nowadays become quickly out of date. Einstein, that great intellectual giant, boasted that he never knew his telephone number but he knew how to find it out.

To a significant extent European awareness already pervades children's lives – the cars they see in the street, the food they see in the supermarkets and above all the programmes they see on television; these all transcend purely national boundaries. To a great extent children live their lives in European space. It is important that schools exploit these natural occurrences of European permeation to help children to attain a growing understanding of what their European citizenship means.

Traditionally of course schools have not mediated a consciousness which transcends national borders. On the contrary, schools in many European countries have been specifically intended to create and sustain a precise national identity both explicitly and implicitly. One of the ways in which national consciousness has been explicitly promoted has been through the teaching of history. Despite developments in the teaching of the subject and despite increasing contact between historians working in different European countries, we are still a long way off realizing the implications of the observation in the French government's response to the 1988 initiative reported in 1992 that: 'L'histoire des nations et des pays de l'Europe ne sont en effet que des points de vue nationaux sur l'histoire Européenne.' ('The history of individual European nations is in fact national views of European history.)

If there is one single historical 'fact' known by every English child and adult it is that William the Conqueror invaded England in 1066 at the Battle of Hastings. If there is one single historical 'fact' known by every French child and adult it is that the English burnt Joan of Arc. In 1988 in this country we celebrated the 400th anniversary of the defeat of the Spanish armada; English children are taught that this was a great victory for the cool-headed Sir Francis Drake. We discovered in 1988 that Spanish history teachers have an entirely different view of a heroic fleet on a mission of justice whose laudable aims were disappointed by bad weather.

These are of course deeply entrenched long-standing national and cultural myths, at least at the level of popular consciousness. It is, though, important to recognize the part played by the teaching of history in sustaining them. During an INSET course on the European dimension at Canterbury Christ Church College a group of teachers compared the accounts of World War I given in two textbooks, one English and one French, widely used in their respective countries to teach 10- to 11-year-olds. The nationalistic tone apparent in both was a striking feature; indeed, one might almost imagine they were not describing the same event. In each account words referring to the nation and its combatants are mentioned six times. No specific mention is made of the French contribution to victory by the British or vice-versa. In fact the only French reference to English soldiers says that they were forced to retreat, whereas French soldiers had a brilliant victory, the 'miracle of the Marne', and held the waves of enemy soldiers back. One third of the British account is given over to the Gallipoli landings and the battles in Jutland, neither of which is mentioned by the French.

The role of history deserves a particular focus because it is one of the most important areas to address if the aims of the European dimension are to be taken seriously. It also illustrates the general task facing all teachers and educators. Providing a European dimension in schooling means taking an in-depth look at the curriculum being offered to school children and asking the question 'Is this what the next generation of Europeans will need?' This question is vitally important for primary schools because they deal with children who are very young and whose attitudes are in the process of being formed. They also deal with children who will not be adult until well into the 21st century, by which time European developments will have evolved still further.

Children need to be prepared for life in what is already to a significant extent a multicultural, multilingual European society. At a conference on the European dimension held in France some years ago a speaker reported on a project carried out by a Parisian primary school which was entitled *Représentations cullinaires*, in the context of an exchange with a school in Sweden. The French children were asked by their teacher to keep a diary of what they ate during one week and at what time they had their meals. This exercise revealed immense diversity within the class. The children said they could not send this information to Sweden as it was not representative of French culture. They decided to send the school menu because this is something they all eat, but then they realized that in the week in question they had eaten Italian pizza on one day and Tunisian couscous on another.

Children need to understand how cultures incorporate elements of other cultures. There is the story of the American boy on holiday in Rome with his parents who observed with delighted surprise: 'Gee Mom, they have pizza in Italy too!' Understanding this process of cultural assimilation and incorporation will help children to confront cultural stereotypes. Stereotypes may contain elements of truth but they distort and deform reality. Children need to know what is false. They need opportunities to get to know children from other European countries through letters and penfriends, electronic technology and visits. Visits need to be well planned so that pupils are prepared to take proper advantage of the experience. They need to be able to see what is there to be seen rather than merely to see what they expect to see. We humans are always ready to notice what we think we know in advance. They need to identify with these common shared elements and to develop a positive attitude towards cultural diversity where differences exist.

Reflecting on the current situation in Europe generally and in education in particular, Shennan (1993) argues that: 'For the young in Europe today a European education is a political, social and economic necessity and an affirmation of their cultural birthright.'

Reflecting on the origins of the post-war development of the European Community, Jean Monet, one of the 'founding fathers', said that if he had to start everything all over again he would not have started with coal and steel but with education. There is no doubt but that the effective teaching of primary MFL can make a vital contribution to the achievement of these ideals, through the central idea of 'inviting' young children to enter into another culture. From the very first lessons, sensitive and thoughtful teaching enables young children to engage personally with a different cultural perspective, to experience it at first hand, 'from the inside'. This direct involvement in the European dimension through 'living the language' helps to build a valuing of multicultural thinking. As Lejeune (1978) notes:

> To aim towards the European dimension of culture does not mean moving away from the culture of one's country or region. Rather the contrary is true. For the road which leads towards others necessarily goes via oneself... As regards culture, enlargement surely implies going deeper down, to the very roots buried in the European soil where we find the collective unconscious from which every European draws sustenance. The personality of the European is enriched by his

becoming aware of his multiple allegiance – city, province, country, Europe – rather than suffer any loss of national identity. The role assigned to the European dimension of culture is precisely that of contributing towards creating this awareness. It is, therefore, vital for us to become familiar with our roots in order to understand that we Europeans are but the branches nourished by the ancient sap of a single tree. The branches differ, the trunk is the same; the countries differ, their origin is the same. This diversity in unity is what makes up Europe.

Primary MFL teaching can begin to help children realize their 'multiple allegiance' and draw on the 'collective unconscious from which every European draws sustenance'. They learn that they can express themselves in a tongue other than that of their mother and do so without feeling that it is alien or peculiar. With good teaching they learn to recognize the commonalities between the target European language and their own first language. For 21st century Europeans facility with at least two European languages and attitudinal comfort in moving between more than two will increasingly become the norm. The process needs to be started young and we turn in the next chapter to the question of who the teachers of this important area should be.

Part 3

The 'who' issues

6
Primary MFL teachers – the specialists or generalists debate

The importance of primary MFL for all pupils

In the last analysis there are really only two ways in which primary MFL can be delivered to pupils as part of the whole curriculum offered within school time. Either the subject is taught by a visiting specialist or it is taught by their own generalist class teacher. Specialists who visit the class to teach the foreign language come in various guises including:

- MFL secondary teachers;
- foreign nationals who happen to be living in the vicinity;
- parents or others from the community who happen to have MFL expertise;
- peripatetics employed by the LEA to implement an authority-wide policy;
- other primary teachers with MFL expertise within the school or a neighbouring school operating on an internal agreement.

The distinctive characteristic of all the specialists is that they have expert knowledge of the subject being taught; the distinctive characteristic of the generalists is that they have a thorough knowledge of the class being taught.

In the present situation of primary MFL teaching in England, however, there is in practice a diverse array of organizational 'models', using specialists and generalists of various kinds in various combinations, through which the subject is delivered. This is inevitable given the arbitrary and unplanned way in which the subject has grown up since 1985. The initiatives that have emerged since then can be grouped under three headings:

● projects initiated and led by LEAs;
● individual primary school initiatives;
● secondary school initiatives with feeder primary schools (including language colleges).

LEA projects vary according to a number of criteria:

● whether there is an inclusive policy of MFL for all primary schools or provision for only some schools;
● whether MFL is provided through additional specialist teachers and what role specialists are intended to play;
● whether there is an intention to train generalist primary class teachers to deliver MFL;
● whether the project is managed specifically by a designated officer;
● whether the scheme directly addresses and involves secondary schools;
● whether there are specific arrangements put in place to provide for continuity and progression across KS2/KS3;
● whether specific resources are allocated including whether a specific scheme of work is designated.

Amongst the LEAs involved in the CILT-directed Good Practice Project referred to in Chapter 3, for example, there is tremendous variation in what is provided to whom, how, why, when and where. Individual primary school initiatives, and those set up by secondary schools with their feeders, are equally multifarious, in terms of the fundamental choices to be made in any local establishment of primary MFL provision in the areas of teaching personnel, training and preparation, roles and responsibilities, aims and objectives, project management, course design, progression and continuity, and so forth.

What needs to be borne in mind in reviewing the current initiatives is that they have all been set up in a context where there is no commitment to universal provision of primary MFL, and that their arrangements and their experiences reflect that fact. These and earlier projects are inherently 'special', and in endeavouring to analyse them for what lessons can be learnt it is important not to lose sight of that special character. In particular, a number of these schemes are expensive and reflect a particular commitment on the part of local policy makers. In a similar way many of the teachers involved in them, both primary and secondary, are also special in the sense that they are likely to have a particular interest and enthusiasm. In planning for universal provision we have to face up to the reality that we are preparing for an 'ordinary' situation which to work well cannot depend on the vagaries of local enthusiasms either to underpin financial generosity or to motivate good quality MFL teaching.

The same point can be made about the schools and other organizations involved in the Good Practice Project. The particular projects eventually selected for funding are by definition special; they are responses to an invitation to bid. In some cases these were projects put together specifically for the Good Practice Project, and as a result the extent to which they are actually examples of good practice or practice which might be generalized really needs to be assessed on a case-by-case basis. They have a very limited time frame in which to be up and running and evaluated. It will be important to learn from projects mounted over a longer period of time in this country and elsewhere. The eventual failure of most LEA programmes based on supernumerary peripatetics, some which had run for decades before running into financial problems, provides a salutary lesson which should not be ignored. Similarly , the Scottish project described earlier can teach us a great deal about how widespread provision of primary MFL can be effectively made.

If the inclusion agenda is really to be met in the case of primary MFL it has to be recognized that the organizational arrangements will not be able to be costly and the teaching will have to be provided as a matter of professional responsibility not just as an expression of interest. And it is not only a question of the inclusion agenda. We do not simply want all children to be taught MFL; we want all children be taught MFL well so that they can progress to higher levels of attainment more quickly. The standards agenda parallels the inclusion agenda in this regard. A major aim of teaching primary MFL is to raise overall standards of achievement in the subject (as argued in Chapter 2) and this cannot be done across the nation as a whole without a proper national system which is not subject to breaks in delivery because funding is suddenly withdrawn or amateur enthusiast teachers move away. Both of these have happened to localized projects in the past decade.

The logical conclusion of all of this is that ultimately it is going to need to be primary teachers themselves who take responsibility for the delivery of primary MFL. Eventually the subject needs to be provided in the same way as any other subject of the primary curriculum. It is the principal contention of this book that worthwhile MFL teaching aimed at raising standards can be provided by primary generalists. This is perhaps not (yet?) a consensus view. Probably the majority of those with any view at all on the subject would still agree with the National Curriculum MFL Working Group position discussed in Chapter 3 that there is simply not enough expertise in the primary teaching force to enable universal provision to be made in this way. However, whatever view one has of the potential of primary teachers to deliver a modern foreign language curriculum, the actual fact of the matter is that in the end universal provision will never be able to be made in any other way. In England there has been and continues to be a chronic shortage of language teachers. Without prohibitively expensive additional investment it is quite impossible to imagine the assembling of an army of MFL specialists to be parachuted into every primary classroom, even if they could be found. This is not a realistic scenario. LEAs which have tried to operate a primary MFL policy on the basis of supernumery peripatetics have mostly had to abandon their schemes in the face of the daunting level of cost involved (eg Tameside, East Sussex, West Sussex). It is highly significant that the Scottish national project described in Chapter 1 has moved away from using visiting specialists towards a reliance on generalists. In the pilot stage of the project 1989–93 the model used was one in which secondary MFL teachers were released to work in primary classrooms with the class teacher present. When the project was extended to the whole country this expensive procedure was abandoned in favour of training primary teachers to undertake the teaching. As Low points out:

> This was a departure from the model of delivery for the MLPS pilot which relied on a partnership between visiting teachers from the modern languages department of the receiving secondary school and primary class teachers in the associated primary schools. The secondary teachers brought their linguistic expertise and the primary class teacher brought their knowledge of appropriate strategies and content for primary-age pupils. The model for the national extension of MLPS would combine these specialist skills in one teacher through a specially designed training course for primary teachers. (Quoted in Driscoll and Frost, 1999: 52.)

The concept of secondary specialists and primary generalists working together in the same classroom clearly strives to maximize the benefits of both to the advantage of pupils. Whether or not this is the best way of delivering primary MFL in practice, the fact of the matter is that it simply cannot be afforded as a permanent basis for national provision.

The Scottish 'solution' then is to have a primary MFL specialist in every school, and this is indeed a move towards the normalization of MFL as a primary curriculum subject. Primary MFL specialists have the potential to operate in a number of ways, and much depends on the nature of the particular primary school within which they work. Where the school is large they may be able to take on the role of specialist and provide MFL teaching of all designated classes. Where they are required to be class teachers the same could be achieved by 'swapping' classes. However, if the effect of this were to take this teacher out from 'his' or 'her' class for a disproportionate amount of time, concerns might be felt about the educational effect on the pupils. The primary MFL specialist would play the part of coordinator for the subject throughout the school, and this could involve organizing and delivering training to primary teacher colleagues within the school, perhaps with the aim of eventually empowering them to take on some of the actual teaching themselves. In this way we arrive back at the basic position that in the long run it is the primary class teacher who needs to be equipped to take at least partial responsibility for the teaching of primary MFL.

The optimistic message this book is attempting to convey is that there is no need in the longer term to be downhearted about this state of affairs. This may be one instance where it is actually possible to make a virtue out of necessity. Primary class teachers are not just the only possible way of giving all pupils the opportunity to begin learning a foreign language, they are also in the end one of the best ways of doing this. While it may appear common sense to think that a specialist teacher with expert knowledge would teach the subject more effectively than a primary teacher with modest levels of ability in the language (although increasingly the younger primary teachers who have experienced the National Curriculum during their secondary schooling may have more than modest competence), in practice the situation is more complex, and as the song has it, 'it ain't necessarily so'.

Advantages and disadvantages of specialist and generalist teaching

Some specialist teachers have no teaching qualification or previous primary teaching experience. Some receive local authority training, guidance and support; others do not. Some participate in a scheme or project, others operate on the basis of individual initiative. Nonetheless it is possible to distil out some specific generic advantages and disadvantages of using specialist teachers.

There are five main advantages:

Excellent expert linguistic role model. Specialist teachers model the language for pupils in a competent and confident manner. MFL is a subject with a strong 'performance' element, in which to a considerable extent the teacher embodies the content to be learnt. Arguably this is different from the situation of the history teacher, say, who is more in the position of 'teaching about' the content of that discipline. Specialist teachers of MFL 'perform' their subject with skill, accuracy, fluency and understanding.

Correct pronunciation and intonation are taught. Specialist teachers know and demonstrate accurate pronunciation of the language. They have authentic sounding accents. They are in a well-founded position to assess and correct pupils' pronunciation and intonation. However, it does need to be borne in mind that unless a person has been brought up with the language they are unlikely ever to reach perfection in this area in the sense of being absolutely indistinguishable from indigenous speakers. Specialist teachers who have learnt the target language through study rather than through natural acquisition, even with experience abroad, do not normally have native command of the language.

Specialist teachers are able to use the target language spontaneously. Despite not necessarily being linguistically perfect, specialist teachers are equipped to use the target language spontaneously in all circumstances without prior planning or preparation. They can in this way show pupils effectively how the language is used for real everyday purposes. Given the emphasis now on the aim of fostering communicative competence, this is an important skill.

Specialist teachers have knowledge of the linguistic and cultural context. Specialist teachers have usually had substantial experience of living in the cultural context in which the target language is spoken and as a result have not only acquired a profound understanding of how things are done and what people typically think, feel and believe, but also have amassed a wealth of insights, stories and anecdotes that can be brought into lessons to help pupils set the language in human perspective. Trained specialist teachers also tend to have a more informed understanding of the structure of the foreign language and are therefore better positioned to respond to and correct pupil error.

Lessons are planned in the context of full knowledge of the target language. Because of their mastery of the above four domains of knowledge and skill specialist teachers of MFL are able to plan, deliver and evaluate lessons on the basis of extensive familiarity with the overall structure of the language. In theory this puts them in a better position to plan thoroughly for progression and continuity.

However, there are three possible disadvantages in having specialist teachers:

Variability in pedagogic expertise. None of the above advantages can actually be turned into real learning and pupil progress without pedagogic expertise. Everybody has met the teacher who knows everything about their subject but who is quite incapable of communicating this to learners. High levels of subject knowledge per se are not a sufficient condition to ensure good teaching and secure learning, a principle which I now realize underpinned some of the less than good teaching I received at the hands of academically well-qualified but untrained grammar school teachers in the 1960s. This is the major difficulty in the use of specialists, especially those who are not themselves qualified teachers. Some primary schools have experienced the unfortunate situation where a French national who happens to be living in the neighbourhood is invited in to 'do a bit of French' but who through lack of teaching skill only manages to alienate the children from the whole business of language learning. Demand for early MFL teaching has recently escalated and a number of commercially based operations have emerged, which in some cases offer primary MFL as an extra-curricular activity. Often these are led by people with some foreign language expertise but little specific teaching expertise. If primary modern languages are badly taught, the job of the secondary school is made all but impossible and it is very easy to teach children to dislike foreign languages. It would be better to do nothing than to end up immunizing whole cohorts of youngsters against MFL learning. There are of course many ways in which training and support can be given (see Chapter 7) but even secondary teachers with Qualified Teacher Status (QTS) are not necessarily adept at managing teacher–pupil interaction in the primary context. As the quotation from Low above suggests, it was seen as beneficial in the Scottish project that secondary teachers drew on the experience of primary teachers in relation to pedagogic method. To be well taught, primary MFL must be firmly secured in primary methodology, culture and ethos.

Outsider status: fragmented teacher–pupil relationships. Specialist teachers deliver their lessons at specific times on specific days. Their relationships with primary pupils are also specific. This situation presents specialist teachers with a number of challenges. It is in some senses at variance with the predominant ambience of primary classrooms, even now in an era where there is more formal timetabling in primary schools than there used to be. As suggested in Chapter 1, primary pupils' learning is characteristically fostered within a friendly, caring and 'communal' atmosphere, where there are deep and rich relationships between classes and their teachers. It can be difficult for external specialists coming in from the outside to be perceived by the children in quite the same intimate way. This is highly significant in the context of a subject like modern languages, where, given the overwhelming emphasis on oral skills set in contexts of social interaction, so much depends upon the quality of the relationship between teacher and taught. If pupils do not respond warmly to the teacher, they are unlikely to respond warmly to the invitation to communicate and all too easily a resistance to the teacher becomes a resistance to the subject. MFL learning requires the pupil to make funny noises, to accept vulnerability, to risk getting things publicly wrong. Trust between teacher and pupil is crucial, and this does not automatically arise in the specialist teaching situation. Again it would be wrong to imply that there are always difficulties. The point at issue, however, is that the very situation of specialists is less well adapted to the conditions ideally in place to maximize the effectiveness of primary MFL teaching.

Inability to integrate the foreign language into the whole curriculum or embed it in pupil experience. Because they come and go, staying only for the lesson, it is not possible for outside specialists teachers to provide for the integration of the foreign language into the primary curriculum and the whole life of the class. This deprives the pupils of what is arguably an absolutely fundamental entitlement in MFL learning to experience it as a pervasive feature of everyday life in school in the way described in Chapters 1 and 4. Never again in the pupil's school career will this opportunity arise. Secondary schools cannot provide it except in exceptional circumstances. Now it is of course possible for the school to decide on an integrationist approach to supplement the specialist lessons, but without the linchpin of the class teacher's personal involvement in the actual teaching of the MFL the effect is diluted. Moreover, the absence of the generalist class teacher from MFL teaching sends an unfortunate message to the pupils. This is a subject their teacher cannot teach, it is different, it is separate. It is not like English, history, or PE. This perception is singularly unhelpful in persuading children of the normalcy of something inherently 'foreign'.

The main advantages of generalist teaching are those implicitly referred to in the above disadvantages of specialist teaching, and which have been set out throughout the chapters of this book. In summary they are: expertise in primary pedagogy; rich relationships with pupils to underpin motivation and learning; and ability to embed and integrate the foreign language into all aspects of classroom life.

The main disadvantages borne by generalists are those deriving from their lack of advanced foreign language knowledge, ie a limited ability to offer a linguistic role model, less secure pronunciation and intonation, and little scope really to use the target language spontaneously. Once again, in common-sense terms it might appear that these are pretty damning weaknesses. There are though a number of important points which need to be taken into account in weighing up all of the advantages and disadvantages of both generalists and specialists. The real issues go beyond common-sense reactions.

The real issues in the specialist and generalist debate

It is important to remember that the actual difference between most non-native specialist and secondary teachers of foreign languages on the one hand, and primary generalists who take on some sort of MFL teaching on the other, is a difference of degree not kind. It is certainly not an absolute difference of perfect knowledge against imperfect knowledge. In working with primary teachers following in-service training courses to support their development into teaching French I have often found that this realization is experienced as a kind of liberation. Implicitly they had often simply taken it for granted that secondary and specialist teachers speak French perfectly. It is reassuring for them to realize that specialist experts are in fact just further on down the same path rather than inhabiting some sort of unattainable secret garden.

This is certainly not to say, of course, that it does not matter whether words are pronounced correctly or sentences are constructed in accordance with the rules of grammar. It matters greatly. What can be said, however, is that provided the language abilities of primary and secondary teachers are appropriately matched to the levels of demand required in their respective pedagogic contexts, a primary practitioner someway back down the path of language learning can nevertheless perform effectively in relation to the needs of the primary context, and do so in a way equivalent to the secondary teacher functioning well with older children. In this manner a significant contribution can be made to raising overall standards of performance in the subject generally. How can this be done?

Firstly, it is essential that the primary MFL curriculum be focused in scope and closely defined (as outlined in Chapter 4). Then the actual language demanded of the teacher can be itemized and mastered. Most primary teachers will have studied a foreign language to age 16. New teachers entering training who have been through secondary schooling since the advent of the National Curriculum in 1988 will all have been taught a foreign language. There is likely therefore in most cases to be a foundation of linguistic knowledge which can be built on. And given appropriate levels of motivation and professional commitment to the task most primary teachers can acquire the necessary knowledge, skills and understanding to deliver this delimited curriculum and the integrationist approach associated with it. In implementing this they draw on high levels of pedagogic skill, which to all intents and purposes they frequently see as simply doing the same sorts of things they do with other subjects anyway.

This is the second important issue. It cannot be too strongly argued that good teaching of MFL in the primary school depends on mastery of effective teaching techniques and the establishment of positive teacher–pupil relationships. Crudely it could be said that there are really only two things which are needed to provide sound primary MFL teaching: linguistic knowledge and pedagogic expertise. Even more crudely it could be said that the situations of generalist and specialist teachers in relation to these two aspects are as shown in Table 6.1.

Table 6.1 Generalist and specialist teachers' linguistic knowledge and pedagogic expertise

	Linguistic knowledge	*Pedagogic expertise*
Specialists	High, flexible	Low, inflexible
Generalists	Low, inflexible	High, flexible

Of course the ideal MFL teacher could thus be said to be the primary generalist who has a specialist background in MFL. Such people are, however, a rare breed, really an endangered species in England ever since the Burstall Report of 1974. For the most part, therefore, a choice has to be made between those who are high on flexibility in relation to language knowledge and those who are high on flexibility in relation to pedagogic expertise. It is my view that the latter should be chosen, a principle described elsewhere (Sharpe, 1995) as the 'primacy of pedagogy'.

In a fascinating research study, which compared the operation of one LEA's primary MFL policy based on the use of supernumary peripatetic specialists with the system established by an adjoining LEA to develop county-wide provision based on training up generalists to work with their own primary classes, Driscoll (1999) found that there were clear differences in the language learning experience provided to pupils. While the linguistic content of lessons in both generalist and specialist programmes was systematically structured into thematic or topic-based units, the specialists' lessons were much more formally organized, with clear boundaries between the introductory phase, the activity phase and the consolidation phase: 'The generalist lessons also consisted of phases but they were much more fluid; frequently the activity and consolidation phases were combined and the assessment was less visible and interwoven into the process of the lesson… [generalists'] lessons were relatively informal with a much slower pace, *mediated by the pupils' understanding.'* (Driscoll, 1999: 33–35.)

This last point was found to be significant throughout the study. The generalists engaged with the pupils as learners much more directly than the specialists, who focused on their syllabus. The anxiety of the external specialists about managing behaviour and discipline was also a pervasive factor. Driscoll found that the specialist teachers tended to concentrate on 'more controlled language activities such as paired role play' and 'promoted more individual work'. One of the specialist teachers commented that 'they get all "up in the air" if we do too many games and songs'. This is quite ironic given that games and songs are so fundamental to good practice in primary MFL teaching. Driscoll observes 'The specialists tended to stick to a predictable format to maintain a sense of discipline, order and quietness.' (Driscoll, 1999: 36–37.)

One consequence of the specialists' greater concern with the subject matter and moving on relatively quickly through the agreed content was that the range of performance between pupils became more extensive, whereas with the generalists, 'pupils returned again and again to the same vocabulary and phrases, in different games and activities and from the early stages of the study it was noticeable that the lower ability pupils were confident, enjoyed French and "felt on a par with the others".' (Driscoll, 1999: 40.)

Given the current emphasis on inclusive education that runs through every aspect of the National Curriculum it can only be concluded from the evidence gathered by Driscoll that the generalist scheme catered better for the whole spectrum of pupil attainment than the specialist strategy. Moreover, there are important implications for the issue of continuity if primary schools allow a situation to develop in which receiving secondary schools cannot build upon a known defined syllabus which they can assume all pupils have more or less mastered before entering KS3 at Year 7. Herein also lies of course the importance of realistic ambitions in the defined curricular content, precisely so that every child can achieve mastery of it.

There is yet a further disadvantage of encouraging the spread and differentiation apparent among the classes taught by specialists. Lower achieving pupils are obviously more likely to become disaffected, and this was seen to add to the discipline difficulties with which the specialists sometimes had to battle. Specialists were more likely to find themselves having to interrupt the progress of the lesson to police pupils' behaviour. As Driscoll notes, 'It was extremely difficult in some cases for the specialist teacher to penetrate the culture in the classroom and gain recognition as a significant member of the group' (Driscoll, 1999: 43.) Sometimes this was made worse by the professional tensions that existed between the class teachers and the incoming external specialist, which Driscoll suggested arose from differences in pedagogical beliefs and values. It may also be due to the 'disempowering' effect described above whereby both pupils and class teacher are aware that this is something the teacher who teaches them everything else cannot do. Driscoll reports an incident in which the class teacher indulged in ostensible humour which probably masked resentment:

T: OK everyone, the franglai woman's here.

T: Time for franglai...

T: Bon juwer tutti li mondi.

Although not always as acrimonious, not to say unprofessional, as this, the whole process of 'handing the class over' to someone from the outside was an issue fraught with uncertainties, anxieties and/or ambiguities that always had to be addressed. The potential for negative feelings to arise in the minds of all three parties concerned – the incoming specialist, the outgoing teacher leaving 'his' or 'her' class, and the pupils themselves – was and is ever present. This does not get the specialist's disciplinary grasp of the pupils in the lesson off to a good start, and in the absence of 'being on the inside', in relation to the culture of the class and detailed insight into individual learners across the curriculum, some struggled and were forced into managing behaviour to some extent at the expense of managing learning.

By contrast the generalists' behaviour control was seen to be quietly effective: 'the generalist teachers used more invisible management strategies, embedded in and underpinned by their relationship with the pupils. The pupils tended to be more compliant and prepared to co-operate and the classroom management tended to be a cheerful, good humoured affair...' (Driscoll, 1999: 42).

It is not difficult to see which of the two disciplinary styles is most conducive to initiating that vital willingness to communicate without which MFL learning objectives simply cannot be achieved. Thus it is possible to argue that the real issues in the specialist/generalist debate are essentially pedagogic rather than linguistic.

The congruence of generalist intentions and the aims of primary MFL

It is perhaps useful at this point to bear in mind quite what these two LEA schemes and primary MFL in general are trying to achieve. One of the secondary teachers interviewed by Driscoll who worked in the LEA where generalist provision had been developed viewed the innovation very positively for the following reason:

> Before they did primary French the children would arrive at the school and I would say nearly every year we had a child who became a school refuser because they were timid and they didn't like speaking... in all subjects, but the reason that would be given was that French was the thing that they were terrified of, having to come in and speak in class. I haven't had that at all from anybody since the primary French came in, and I think the reason is that they have got over that in a nice cosy atmosphere in their primary school with all their mates, with a teacher they know... and they are a lot more confident. (Driscoll, 1999: 13)

Consider the following aims:

- What we want to do is to ensure that primary-age children have a positive and enjoyable experience of learning foreign languages.
- We want this linked in to the total primary curriculum and the child's whole school experience.
- We want this for all children and we do not want so unrealistic a curriculum that it creates wide differentiation before entry into the secondary cycle.
- We want children to feel the urge to learn more about foreign languages when they get there and strive for progress because they feel confident and secure in their learning.
- We want sound and secure understanding in the early stages which will contribute to the raising of standards of achievement.

If we can agree these points, then it seems clear that primary MFL learning is best achieved by training and empowering primary class teachers to deliver it to their own pupils.

In the Kent scheme (Sharpe, 1995; Rumley and Sharpe, 1999) for example, ordinary primary class teachers were turned into primary MFL teachers by the following eight means:

- The provision of user-friendly audio-visual resources designed for the non-specialist.
- Supportive but demanding CPD/INSET sessions involving modelling of specific lessons.
- Encouraging teachers to apply their existing primary pedagogic skills to this new subject area.
- Encouraging teachers to integrate the MFL into the whole curriculum.
- Encouraging teachers to embed foreign language utterances in everyday activities.
- Encouraging the extensive use of games and songs.
- The appointment of a primary MFL advisor to provide county-wide coordination, coherence and support.
- The provision of specialist/native speakers (including foreign language assistants) as resources in the primary MFL classroom.

Taken together these measures go some considerable way to alleviating the weakness of generalists in relation to the important task of modelling the language. It is certainly important that primary pupils hear the foreign language fluently spoken with correct pronunciation and intonation. It is less certainly important that they hear nothing but the fluent speaking of the target language. It has already been argued above that it is not necessarily an unmitigated benefit to learning to have everything in the lesson done in the target language, even though the general arguments for teaching as much as possible in the foreign language are clearly valid. Through using audio and video material, authentic language available through the Internet, native and other MFL specialists as resources, the primary teacher can ensure that pupils are exposed to excellence in 'performance' of the foreign language.

It is important to be clear that 'supported generalists' can in this way deliver an early teaching programme of language acquisition of the kind set out in the syllabus described in Chapter 4 which goes way beyond mere 'language awareness' or sensitization in the sense of the *apprentissage/sensibilisation* debate (see Chapter 2). What these generalists are doing is teaching specific aspects of the KS3 MFL curriculum during KS2. Kent LEA has been working with primary generalists for the past 10 years or so and has a primary MFL scheme which is applied countywide. Ofsted inspections of its schools have in recent years included inspections of the quality of French teaching, and the published reports arising from these inspections have been markedly positive not just about the confidence and enthusiasm of pupils but also about the specific linguistic standards of achievement they reach. These reports are in the public domain and available from the Ofsted Web site. In one school inspectors judged that 'Good progress is made by most pupils within the short time allocated. Higher attaining and confident pupils make very good progress. Pronunciation and levels of grammatical accuracy are generally high.'

In another school it was noted that 'All pupils, including those with special education needs, attain well and make good progress at both key stages... The subject enhances pupils' understanding of cultural diversity, supports the literacy and numeracy programme and has links with information technology... Pupils communicate confidently in French as they progress through the school and they show respect for the oral contributions of other pupils.'

In yet another school the conclusion was that 'Across the school pupils make good progress. They build on basic vocabulary learnt in YR (Reception Year) and develop this as they make progress through the school so that they can hold class discussions in some detail in French. Their growing confidence enables pupils to use increasingly complex vocabulary and they are beginning to recognise many written words.'

These Ofsted judgements are evidence that primary generalist teachers can provide valuable learning experiences in MFL for their pupils. At the same time of course equally fulsome praise can be found in Ofsted reports on primary schools where the teaching is provided by specialists, and in the present situation this diversity of provision is likely to continue. In particular some very good work is being done by language colleges working with clusters of feeder primary schools. The difficulty is that by definition language colleges will always be a minority of secondary schools and a national system cannot be based on this level of cross-phase support and resourcing. In writing about the Scottish initiative, Giovanazzi (1992) firmly declared: 'The purpose of our teaching languages in primary school is language competence not awareness... nor is our pilot project seen as simply being a preparation for the "more serious" work of secondary school. The primary school may be the beginning of language learning, but it is no mere "softening up" process.'

If the above Ofsted comments about pupil performance were judgements of a national system of primary MFL teaching in England as a whole rather than of individual schools in its south-east corner, the hopes and aspirations of many of the subject's advocates would be well on the way to being realized. In the next chapter issues involved in providing initial and in-service teacher training to support a national scheme are considered.

7

Primary MFL teachers – education, training and professional development

Teacher supply in primary MFL

Given that ultimately there are only two possible options for staffing the provision of modern language teaching in primary schools, ie the use of specialists or of generalists as discussed in the previous chapter, it follows that arrangements for the training of teachers of primary MFL need, ideally, to provide for both. This is really only to say once again that MFL ought to be treated in the same way as other subjects of the primary curriculum, where initial teacher training programmes are designed to produce generalist class teachers who have the capacity to cover most or all of the primary curriculum, as well as specialists who can provide leadership in relation to the teaching of their subject throughout the school, as well as engaging in specialist teaching themselves.

In England there are very few trained specialist primary teachers of modern foreign languages. Essentially the supply of primary MFL specialists dried up after the perceived failure of the 1960s/1970s project, as explained in Chapter 1. With a handful of exceptions most teacher training institutions abandoned MFL as a specialist subject for primary teacher trainees. Legislation enacted during the 1990s imposed increasingly specific prescriptions on the content of teacher training courses and this tended to reinforce the exclusion of MFL as a subject for primary trainees. Applicants for primary initial teacher training (ITT) are required to specialize in a National Curriculum subject. At both undergraduate and postgraduate levels some applicants may enter with expertise in a foreign language, but they cannot treat this as their specialist subject. This absolute ban was partially lifted in

2000 by the decision of the Teacher Training Agency and the Department for Education in England to set aside a small number of teacher training places for primary MFL as part of the government's Early Language Learning Initiative, discussed earlier. The hope is that this process will begin to produce a corps of primary MFL specialists, but the numbers are small and its effects will only be felt in the longer term. The basic position remains that ITT is about preparing intending teachers to teach the sacred pantheon of the National Curriculum, where for the moment primary MFL has no place.

Thus the present situation of bottom–up growth in primary MFL teaching is characterized by having either MFL specialists of some kind without primary teacher training or trained primary teachers without a thorough knowledge of MFL as a discipline. Furthermore, this has happened at a time of growing shortages in the supply of secondary MFL teachers. The subject appears to have become less and less popular with secondary school pupils, of whom a diminishing number subsequently seek to become teachers of the subject.

Therefore in practice the reference to 'specialists' of some kind connotes a broad array of types of teacher, among whom we might number:

- Secondary trained specialist MFL teachers who may seek employment as specialist MFL teachers in one or more primary schools, possibly in England under LEA schemes.
- Specialist MFL teachers from neighbouring secondary schools who by arrangement teach classes in some of their feeder primaries.
- Secondary trained specialist MFL teachers who find employment in primary schools (maybe through phase retraining) and may operate as 'semi-specialists' taking some colleagues' classes for MFL on an exchange basis;
- Native speakers who are not trained teachers but who are employed by schools to teach their mother tongue in curriculum time.
- Native speakers who may or may not be trained teachers but who employ themselves or are employed by external organizations to provide language learning opportunities for primary pupils outside school hours in extra-curricular 'French clubs' and the like.
- Diverse MFL peripatetics, such as MFL graduates, who may not have undergone teacher training of any sort.
- Specialist primary MFL teachers who followed a course of primary initial teacher education in which the subject was either a main or a subsidiary area of study.

Apart from the final category, there are training issues for all categories of teacher presently undertaking primary MFL teaching, including obviously the primary generalists discussed in Chapter 6. We might say that there are supply problems for all human resources (HR) aspects of primary and secondary MFL teaching. In 1990 the House of Lords debated the teaching of foreign languages in primary schools. Baroness Lockwood observed: 'the two main problems affecting modern foreign language learning in the United Kingdom are the current crisis in teacher supply and the widespread lack of motivation and interest in foreign languages' (House of Lords Report, 1990: 562).

This overall position has remained unchanged into the 21st century. It is notable that the major professional association for foreign language teachers, the Association for Language Learning, has toned down the enthusiasm of its earlier 1992 policy on the issue of primary MFL, to advocate instead that inclusion of MFL in the primary curriculum for all pupils should be seen as 'a long-term target' in order to allow time for:

- initial teacher training in primary MFL;
- revision of National Curriculum requirements;
- publishers to develop new course books;
- in-service training/continuing professional development (CPD) to train primary generalists in MFL;
- in-service training/CPD to train secondary MFL specialists in primary methodologies.

This more cautious approach, of developing a strategic plan before formal inclusion of the subject in the primary curriculum, reflects the serious training and supply questions which face advocates of an earlier start to MFL teaching. Sceptics certainly fear that seeking to recruit more primary MFL specialists might make the dire shortage of secondary MFL specialists even worse. In point of fact, however, the motivations of applicants for each phase may be entirely different, and if more primary MFL places in ITT were offered it would not necessarily mean that even fewer applications would be made for ITT in secondary MFL.

The context of ITT in England

The establishment of the Teacher Training Agency in 1994 began a process of radical reform of teacher training in England. Governments of the mid- and late-1990s felt that to carry forward the school reforms of the late 1980s and early 1990s it was necessary to reconfigure and redefine the process through which teachers were to be prepared to assume their professional responsibilities. By the turn of the 20th century the following key principles were firmly in place (see for example DfEE Circulars 10/97 and 4/98):

- ITT must be grounded firmly in the practitioner context: schools must be involved fully in the planning, delivery and monitoring of teacher training courses, either in the context of School Centred Initial Teacher Training (SCITT) programmes or in partnership with institutions of higher education.
- Clearly defined detailed standards for the award of QTS need to be set by the Secretary of State for Education which all teacher trainees must demonstrate before being allowed into the profession.
- Many QTS standards are common to both the primary and secondary phases; others are phase specific;
- National Curricula for initial teacher training are needed to prescribe what must be known and understood by teacher trainees over and above the National Curriculum for schools which they are required to teach.

During the 1990s a lot of ideas about how teachers should be trained, which had tended to be taken for granted before, were made explicit. And perhaps because these ideas had been rather taken for granted they had not always been thought through or thought about as fully as they should have been. It seems obvious that schools should play an important part in the training of future members of the teaching profession, yet before partnership was made a specific requirement for providers of teacher training, subject to inspection by Ofsted, the extent of their involvement was highly variable. Similarly, it may seem self-evident that intending teachers should show that they have the necessary skills and knowledge to do the job before being given accreditation for a life-long career, but here too there was enormous variability in practice prior to the definition of national standards.

All types of ITT are essentially concerned with two elements. First, subject knowledge – does the teacher trainee have the knowledge, skills and understanding to secure mastery of the subject content they are expected to teach to pupils? Second, subject application – does the teacher trainee have the knowledge, skills and understanding to teach the subject content effectively?

The question for us here is what it is that ITT courses need to provide in terms of subject knowledge and subject application for those who want to teach primary MFL.

Primary MFL and ITT

The possible types or levels of provision of ITT in primary MFL are analysed below:

1. MFL graduate enters a primary PGCE/SCITT course.
2. Graduate in another subject with some MFL knowledge enters a primary PGCE/SCITT course.
3. During undergraduate primary ITT course (BEd, etc) trainee takes MFL as major specialism.
4. During undergraduate primary ITT course or PGCE course trainee takes MFL as non-specialist subject study.
5. During undergraduate or PGCE course trainee covers MFL as part of general primary curriculum studies.

Against regulations at the time of writing candidates are required for major specialisms to have 'secure knowledge of the subject to at least a standard approximating to GCE 'A' level in those aspects of the subject taught at KS1 and KS2.' This applies to the first three types of trainee listed above. Type 4 teacher trainees must have 'secure knowledge to a standard equivalent to at least level 7 of the pupils' national curriculum'. There are no specifications for type 5.

We need to consider what kinds of subject knowledge and subject application are appropriate for each of these levels of provision. In each case trainees will need different kinds of learning experience to enhance their subject knowledge and their understanding of its application to the classroom context.

However, we also need to be clear what is meant by subject knowledge in the case of primary MFL. Some might argue that the subject knowledge required is native mastery of the language. There are, however, two objections to this view. The first is that native mastery alone is not enough. MFL subject knowledge also means explicit, overt knowledge of the foreign language in question, which is a different matter from simply being able to speak or write it. Secondly, the majority of MFL specialists in England and in other countries are not native speakers of the language they teach. Yet many of them are excellent teachers who teach pupils extremely well.

In a similar way, subject application is not just about teaching the subject. In order to teach any subject well it is necessary to have a sound grasp of the teaching learning process generally.

These elements of subject knowledge and subject application are represented in Figure 7.1.

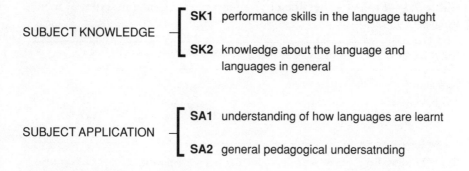

SUBJECT KNOWLEDGE

SK1 performance skills in the language taught

SK2 knowledge about the language and languages in general

SUBJECT APPLICATION

SA1 understanding of how languages are learnt

SA2 general pedagogical undersatnding

Figure 7.1 The relationship between the elements of subject knowledge and subject application in effective modern language teaching (Sharpe, 1999)

These four elements are analytically distinct but mutually interrelated in practice. They are all necessary if effective MFL teaching is to occur. Figure 7.1 shows the position of native speakers who may well only be operating in SK1. It indicates why schools who take in untrained native speakers to offer a foreign language to pupils have sometimes found that things do not work out well. Native speakers, such as foreign language assistants, are a magnificent resource for any MFL teacher, primary or secondary, but what the French call 'responsabilité pedagogique' should never be abdicated. The resource is not the teacher.

Putting together this analysis of what trainee teachers in primary MFL need to master with the various types of trainee defined earlier we can identify the profile of training needs of each, as shown in Table 7.1.

In relation to training in SK1 there two basic areas which need to be addressed. ITT providers need to ensure that trainees acquire a knowledge of the kind of foreign language content covered in the primary phase, and they need to prepare trainees to use the language for real purposes in the classroom, preferably spontaneously to express ideas as they occur. In the present state of primary MFL teaching, as described in previous chapters, there is great variation in the substantive content taught to pupils. However, the approach to be taken is that the non–specialists, even in type 5 above, should as a minimum be able to manage the limited linguistic demands made by a syllabus such as that presented in Chapter 4. Equally, it is to be expected that their ability to use the language spontaneously will have limitations, but even from a restricted repertoire some situationally appropriate choices can be made which bring the language to life. For specialists the problem is often the

Table 7.1   Profile of the different training needs of different types of trainee (Sharpe, 1999)

Trainee type	SK1	SK2	SA1	SA2
Specialists				
PG MFL graduate or native speaker	should be secure	build on established understanding	specific training	GPS course needed
PG MFL subsidiary subject in degree	may need developing	specific training needed	specific training needed	GPS course neede
UG MFL main subject	develop to A level+	main focus of training	main focus of training	GPS course needed
Non specialists				
UG or PG with MFL option	develop to NC level 7	subsidiary focus of training	subsidiary focus of training	GPS course needed
UG or PG with MFL in curriculum studies	basic structures	—— application of general principles ——		

PG = postgraduate   UG = undergraduate   GPS = general professional studies

reverse. Certainly for native speakers and MFL graduates there should be no difficulty in using the language in everyday interactions. But it is important for able and competent linguists to be sensitive to the difficulties posed by foreign language structures for young learners. Because they have had to learn the language as a foreign language indigenous MFL graduates may empathize with the difficulties their pupils experience. Such empathetic understanding can be harder for native speakers, who may not automatically see how to make appropriate linguistic selections for primary pupils.

Postgraduate primary students taking a specialism in MFL should have their competence in the language audited. The principle that ITT providers are responsible for the levels of subject knowledge which their trainees demonstrate is well established now. It is not unknown for undergraduates to have a developed appreciation of literature but weaknesses in other areas of the language. A perennial difficulty with all PGCE courses is the lack of time available. So much needs to be compressed into so short a course (currently 38 weeks, of which 18 weeks are spent in schools). It is often effective to identify learning needs and then to make the trainees themselves responsible for addressing it by pointing them to resources and learning opportunities available in the institution.

For undergraduate students who are acquiring the language at the same time as undergoing teacher training the SK1 element needs to be an integral and ongoing part of the whole course. Time abroad in a country where the chosen language is spoken should be built in to the programme where at all possible. Given the extent to which the teaching of primary MFL has developed on the European mainland it is becoming progressively easier to locate partner ITT institutions in European countries willing to engage in reciprocal exchange arrangements. While not needing to reach native command, MFL specialists do need always to bear in mind that there is a 'performance' element to their subject. In this sense they are in a similar position to teachers of art, music and physical education. However, in these areas it is acknowledged that teachers can coach students to deliver higher standards of performance than they themselves can reach. This is much more difficult to imagine in MFL. Successful MFL teachers may only be one step ahead of their pupils in the language studied, but they do need to be ahead!

Much SK2 learning arises naturally in the course of SK1 language learning. This does give some additional benefit to the concurrent undergraduate route where issues of SK1 and SK2 can be consciously considered in tandem. Well-planned ITT courses can ensure that these two elements are integrated in a mutually reinforcing and holistic manner. Indeed, they can both be linked also with SA1, so that trainees are thinking about how children learn the language at the same time as they are learning the language.

A major issue for primary ITT providers is to decide what to include in SA1, which is treated as specific to the subject, and what to include in SA2, which is common to all students. While issues covered in general professional studies such as behaviour management, teaching strategies, assessment, recording and reporting clearly have a generalized application, they also have particular applications in each area of the curriculum. In the case of MFL there is the happy circumstance that good practice in the discipline and good practice in primary methodology generally share much in common – visual display, interactive learning, practical activities, etc. Even the more recent shifts in thinking about primary practice – the value of whole class teaching, memorization, repetition, etc – still resonate with useful approaches in MFL teaching.

Training needs of non-specialists

If primary MFL is eventually to be made a statutory requirement, it will not be enough simply to have a corps of primary MFL specialists. Non-specialists primary practitioners will need to be able to deliver the subject as well, just as they do for other subjects of the primary curriculum. Their training needs are in some ways the mirror image of those of the untrained native speaker. Primary generalists have the required pedagogic understanding but not the language facility. Four main objectives need to be built into initial and in-service training for them in primary MFL:

- acquiring secure knowledge of basic structures and vocabulary to underpin:
  - effective real use of the MFL in routine events in the classroom;
  - teaching of linguistic elements within a planned scheme of work;
- acquiring a rudimentary knowledge of the underpinning culture;
- developing a positive and enthusiastic attitude towards MFL teaching/learning;
- applying known principles of good primary pedagogy to MFL.

The attitudinal component of these objectives is of great importance. MFL is an area where 'horses can be taken to troughs of water' without any imbibing happening. Pupils can be obliged to be present at a foreign language lesson but it is not possible to force them to desire to communicate. Still less will they desire to communicate if their teacher's heart is not in it either. In many ways this is the prime concern of in-service courses in MFL for primary teachers. Trainers need to cultivate in them a fervour for the primary MFL teaching project. All non-specialist primary teachers could potentially be trained to conduct ordinary class routines in a foreign language – taking the dinner register, collecting dinner money, lining up, writing the date, distributing or collecting books and files, celebrating birthdays, setting the weather board, etc. All non-specialist primary teachers could use the foreign language to denote classroom objects in daily use. The absorption of foreign vocabulary is in any case a naturally occurring process. What is the difference between talking about visiting the *café* or the *coiffeur* in everyday English and a primary teacher deliberately asking pupils to undertake a written exercise in their *cahier d'histoire* or the *classeur?* Anyone can learn to do this. It just takes the will to do it.

Many of the in-service/CPD training courses primary teachers attend are run in their own time outside school hours. If the teaching of primary MFL in England is eventually to be extended to all pupils, it will likely be necessary to offer longer and more in-depth courses to primary teachers, such as those which have been offered in other countries. In the Scottish experiment, for example, teachers were offered a 27-day course equivalent to 160 hours over a 12-month period. In Italy in-service courses have varied from 'short' courses of 100 hours to 'long' courses of 500 hours. The Scottish training programmes were well received largely because they were perceived to be relevant directly to the primary curriculum rather than being a diluted version of the secondary curriculum. As Martin (2000) comments, they attempted to 'combine within one teacher the specialist linguistic skills of the MFL teacher and the primary teacher's knowledge of appropriate strategies and content for the primary school.' In the next chapter some of the synergies between MFL and primary teaching are explored further.

Part 4

The 'how' issues

8
Primary pedagogy and MFL teaching

Good practice in primary pedagogy

The primary years are an exciting time for children. They have emerged from the gentle infant years of exploration and discovery with developed powers of language and learning, but have not yet arrived at the storm and stress of turbulent adolescence. The world is a fascinating place and they are characteristically eager to find out about it. Beginning to teach in the early 1970s, I was exhorted by local authority advisers to make the classroom 'a place of wonder', and to seek to 'make real' the topics I was teaching in mathematics, history, RE, etc. This is currently not a particularly fashionable emphasis. The present movers and shakers in education policy are more driven by an urgent anxiety to ensure that the nation's competitive edge in the global market is sustained through prescribed literacy and numeracy strategies. And yet the essential point is that inspiring wonder and good teaching of English and mathematics are not mutually exclusive alternatives but in fact complementary activities. It remains to be seen whether the experience of hundreds of literacy hours day after day really will of themselves improve the nation's position in the fierce battleground of economic competition. But one thing is certain: where they work well it will surely be because of good teaching which does seriously engage learner interest, motivation and commitment.

For primary-age children particularly the teacher–pupil relationship is crucial to their progress. At the heart of good primary pedagogy lies the imperative to use that close relationship to stimulate a positive involvement in learning on the part of the child. It is the quality of the teacher–pupil relationship which fundamentally determines the intensity of that involvement, whatever the particular teaching method being employed. In recent years primary teaching methods have become considerably politicized, with ideological battle lines being drawn between the advocates of 'progressive' and 'traditional' approaches. These are often represented as being two opposing poles of a dichotomy, whereas in fact they are very loose terms which each cover a range of pedagogic activities which can be done well or badly. The crucial distinction is not between progressive and traditional, but rather between good and bad teaching.

Mr Thomas Gradgrind in Charles Dickens' *Hard Times* gives us a well-known example from fiction of traditional teaching and rote learning. Sissy Jupe, who has been brought up with horses in the fairground where her father's job is horse-breaking, is unable to respond to Mr Gradgrind's command that she give a definition of a horse. His reaction is instructive:

'Girl number twenty unable to define a horse!... Girl number twenty possessed of no facts, in reference to one of the commonest of animals!...'
'Bitzer,' said Thomas Gradgrind. 'Your definition of a horse.'
'Quadruped. Gramnivorous. Forty teeth, namely twenty-four grinders, four eye-teeth and twelve incisive. Sheds coat in the Spring; in marshy countries, sheds hoofs, too. Hoofs hard, but requiring to be shod with iron. Age known by marks in mouth.'
'Now girl number twenty,' said Mr Gradgrind, 'you know what a horse is.'

Sissy Jupe of course already knows what a horse is, although one wonders whether Bitzer does! Yet Thomas Gradgrind does not engage with her as a learner at all. He takes no account of her existing understanding and does not seek to link what he wants her to know with anything she can perceive as remotely familiar.

One of the central tenets of progressive education is of course precisely the importance of adopting a 'child-centred' approach. Here the idea is that each child is an individual and learning experiences provided by the teacher need to take as their starting point the interests and needs of the child in all his or her uniqueness. This led to ideas such as 'discovery learning', where pupils are invited to explore topics and themes which arouse their curiosity and motivation. Another teacher from literature, Miss Beale in Jan Mark's (1976) delightful 'Thunder and Lightenings', provides an example of how this sometimes worked out in practice. Andrew, a new boy who has just arrived in the class, is introduced by Miss Beale to Victor.

'Miss Beale said you would show me round, to look at the projects,' said Andrew.
'Why, do you want to copy one?, asked Victor, lifting a strand of hair and

exposing one eye. 'You could copy mine, only someone might recognise it. I've done that three times already.'

'Whatever for?' said Andrew. 'Don't you get tired of it?'

Victor shook his head and his hair.

'That's only once a year. I did that two times at the junior school and now I'm doing that again,' he said. 'I do fish, every time. Fish are easy. They're all the same shape.'

'No they're not,' said Andrew.

'They are when I do them,' said Victor. He spun his book round, with one finger, to show Andrew the drawings. His fish were not only all the same shape, they were all the same shape as slugs. Underneath each drawing was a printed heading: BRAEM; TENSH CARP; STIKLBAK; SHARK. It was the only way of telling them apart. The shark and the bream were identical except that the shark had a row of teeth like tank traps.

'Isn't there a 'c' in stickleback?' said Andrew. Victor looked at his work.

'You're right. He crossed out both 'k's, substituted 'c's and pushed the book away, the better to study it. 'I got that wrong last year'...

'Don't you have to write anything?' asked Andrew.

'Yes, look. I wrote a bit back here. About every four pages will do,' said Victor. 'Miss Beale, she keep saying I ought to write more but she's glad when I don't. She's got to read it. Nobody can read my writing.'

There is little evidence here of autonomous, committed, effective individual learning, still less of anything being taught. In practice Andrew and Victor are not learning any better than Sissy Jupe. In Miss Beale's classroom there is no more engagement with learning than there is in Mr Gradgrind's. His demand that pupils memorize arid abstractions does little or nothing to extend their understanding. Miss Beale's pupils learn more about avoiding work than they do about the subject of their 'projects'. Both teachers are dreadful failures who waste their pupils' time. The fact that one of them is using 'traditional methods' and the other 'progressive' methods shows the sheer irrelevance of this much vaunted dichotomy.

Since the Cockroft Report on the teaching of mathematics in 1982 it has become commonplace to list teaching strategies in a sort of 'taxonomy' of different effective ways in which teachers can engage with pupils to teach and bring about learning. The current Ofsted handbook updates this list to include the following:

- exposition;
- explanation;
- demonstration;

- discussion;
- practical activity;
- investigation;
- testing;
- problem solving.

It is therefore not so much a question of using didactic instruction or discovering methods as ensuring a proper balance of activities to promote learning and making certain that these are done well. In each of the pedagogic activities listed above what matters most is that the primary teacher does what is necessary to orientate the learners' will and attention so that they can concentrate actively, whether they are required to listen carefully, as in the first four, or to undertake specific tasks, as in the latter four. For the primary teacher of MFL the two spectres of Mr Gradgrind and Miss Beale loom as ever-present possibilities. Presenting a foreign language always carries with it the risk of Gradgrindian pupil incomprehension. And using a foreign language in pupil activity such as game playing or role-play always risks the possibility of Bealean disengagement from the assigned task. It is clear that in this subject more than others, eliciting pupil loyalty and commitment is of critical importance.

Primary pedagogy and cognitive development

Primary teaching in England was hugely influenced during the mid-20th century by the work of Jean Piaget. He studied how children grow and develop in understanding themselves and their world, and the central proposition of his theory was that child development occurs in a series of clear and distinct stages. These have become famous in the folklore of teachers and educationists:

Sensori-motor stage	(0–2 years)
Pre-operational thought	(2–7 years)
Concrete operations	(7–11 years)
Formal operations	(11 years upwards)

While Piaget's work provided valuable insights into how children think and develop concepts at different ages, the developmental stages theory came under strong criticism in the 1970s and 1980s. In the light of evidence and ideas advanced by other researchers it appeared to present an unnecessarily limited view of what young children are actually capable of. In particular, Noam Chomsky had shown that young children were able to deduce the complex underlying structural and grammatical rules of their mother-tongue languages and generate new completely new linguistically correct sentences that they had never heard before. His famous concept of the 'language acquisition device' suggested that children are born with an in-built capacity to learn a language. Chomsky's argument was mainly with associationist and behaviourist theorists of learning, which asserted that children learn through stimulus–response habit formation. This, he pointed out, could never account for how very young children are able to understand and use language which they have not encountered.

Primary teachers therefore found themselves presented with contradictory evidence about what young children could be expected to achieve. On the one hand Piaget appeared to have shown that the young child could not even imagine what an object might look like from the side which could not be seen, could not understand that quantities of fluids or solids retained the same volume or mass when they changed shape, could not follow the logic that if rod A is longer than rod B, and rod B is longer than rod C, then rod A must also be longer than rod C, and so on. Yet Chomsky appeared to have demonstrated that the young child can master the seemingly vastly more difficult complexities of any known language before the age of three.

A highly influential resolution of this dilemma came with a group of researchers around Margaret Donaldson. Their studies indicated that Chomsky's 'language acquisition device' should be understood as one application of a much more general 'capacity for making sense of certain types of situation involving direct and immediate human interaction'. Donaldson (1991: 37) illustrates this point with an anecdote:

> An Englishwoman is in the company of an Arab woman and her two children, a boy of seven and a little girl of 13 months who is just beginning to walk but is afraid to take more than a few steps without help. The Englishwoman speaks no Arabic, the Arab woman and her son speak no English. The little girl walks to the Englishwoman and back to her mother. Then she turns as if to start off in the direction of the Englishwoman once again. But the latter now smiles, points to the boy and says: 'walk to your brother this time.' At once the boy, understanding the situation, though he understands not a word of the language, holds out his arms. The baby smiles, changes direction and walks to her brother. Like the older child, she appears to have understood the situation perfectly.

And by rerunning some of Piaget's well-known experiments with children in different situations designed to make 'human sense' of them, quite different results were obtained which clearly indicated that young children were much more able to think through, understand and respond to cognitive demands than Piagetian theory suggested. For example, instead of Piaget's questions about what mountains look like from the other side, Martin Hughes constructed a scene in which children had to say whether a doll, who represented a little boy trying to escape from a policeman by hiding, could or could not be seen by the policeman when located in different positions (Donaldson, 1978: 20). The contextualization of the cognitive problem of judging who could see what in a situation where two complementary human intentions were in play, the intention to escape and hide on the one hand and the intention to chase and capture on the other, enabled the children to demonstrate the ability to 'decentre' (ie imagine the situation from someone else's point of view) and to reveal a much higher level of cognitive development than Piaget's findings implied. Thus Donaldson and her colleagues contend that children's capacity to acquire language quickly and their ability to interpret situations result in fact from the same generic cognitive capacity to make sense of human social interaction.

The implications for primary education of this view of how children think are far reaching. Piaget is surely not the only researcher or teacher who has wrongly assumed that children are incapable of something when in fact it was the situation he created himself which produced the results he got. This highlights the importance of setting primary teaching of any subject in contexts with which young children can identify. It means being sensitive continuously to pupil response in order to understand what sense is being made of the teaching. Alison Hurrell, who has played a key role in the Scottish primary MFL initiative, recounts a relevant sobering experience:

> I was telling the story of the little elephant (based loosely on the Rudyard Kipling story) to a class of 10-year-olds. The various animals in the story were introduced – le petit elephant, la girafe, le lion, le singe, le serpent, le crocodile – and the children seemed to be following the storyline, evidenced by group chorusing of key repeated structures and phrases, accompanying hand gestures, smiles and so forth. At the end of the story, one perplexed child asked why all the animals had been phoning each other. It took me some time to realize that for her, le petit elephant had been understood as le petit telephone, and her construction of the story thereafter had been based on that initial misunderstanding. (Hurrell, 1999: 69)

It means above all taking account of the 'holistic' way in which primary-age children understand the world. To promote learning the primary teacher must engage with the cognitive framework the child is using to interpret what is happening in lessons. This is why it is so important in introducing MFL into the primary classroom to present the new language in situations of 'human sense' and as far as possible to include the foreign language in ordinary activities which are part of ongoing social interaction. As Hurrell (1996: 53) comments on the basis of her long experience of primary MFL in Scotland: 'When the foreign language can be linked to other aspects of the primary curriculum, it enables the children to relate the foreign language to concepts of the world they already possess, to make links between the foreign language and language(s) they already possess, to approach their foreign language holistically.'

Good practice in primary MFL teaching

Thus the big advantage of the primary school in a language learning context is that the foreign language can be embedded in the whole experience of the pupil. In this way the subject comes to make 'human sense' to young children. In particular, class teachers can normalize the foreign language by using it for ordinary everyday events and by bringing it into other subjects of the primary curriculum (see Chapter 3). In her unpublished PhD research into the ways in which primary generalists actually used this opportunity, Driscoll observes that:

> The relatively simple, 'routinised' classroom commands such as *levez vous* and *posez vos crayons* were frequently used, as were purposeful routine activities which required small amounts of the large language such as taking the register. The extract below is a typical example of how the generalist teachers took the register at least once a week, outside of lesson time.

> T: Bonjour tout le monde. Brrr, il fait froid, n'est-ce pas? Please put your projects on the table, and then get ready for your groups (the children were divided into ability groups for the core subjects and moved classes). En Français, s'il vous plait.
> T: Mary?
> P: Oui, Madame.
> T: Helen?
> Ps: Elle est absente.
> T: Qu'est-ce qu'elle a?
> Ps: Elle est malade.
> T: Peter?
> P: Il est malade.
> T: Peut-être qu'il est absent, peut-être qu'il est en retard.
> *(Register then called for the whole class.)*
> T: Bon, alors qu'est-ce qu'on va manger aujourd'hui?
> T: Patrick?

P: Je vais manger un sandwich à l'école.
T: Daniel?
P: Je vais manger le déjeuner à l'école.
Etc.
T: Get all your things ready for the maths swap.

Driscoll argues that much of the success she found in motivating high levels of interest and application was due to the sheer quality of the teaching demonstrated by the primary generalists across the whole curriculum.

They have a wealth of experience in organising practical activities in Art or PE efficiently and safely, and so little curriculum time is lost. These organisational strategies prove to be a real advantage for the generalist because it permitted the use of all manner of materials and resources throughout the entire school. They were thus able to offer a multi-sensory experience in teaching French that was not only interesting and motivating, but highly effective in the memorisation of facts such as numbers up to 100.

By drawing on this established professional expertise in the primary practitioner context generalist teachers were able to operate effectively as teachers of MFL, even though their knowledge of the subject did not approach that of the specialist. In the following account of a lesson centred on personal information, Driscoll underlines the positive language learning environment the teacher is able to create.

Before she gave out the 'identity cards' she waited for silence, and for each child to give her their full attention. There was a level of anticipation of the fun activity they were about to do. The children knew from previous experience that any sign of uncooperative behaviour might result in the French being cancelled for another day.

T: Today we're going to change our identity, a new age a new name. It may not be where you really live. I'm going to come around and tell you how to pronounce your new names.
The children received about 6 cards, and started to wander around the class.
T: When you've found someone who is the same age, stick together. Trouver les personnes avec les mêmes ages que vous.
Although this appears to be a practice exercise of phrases already learnt, in fact the dimension of the game means the teacher and pupil interact for a real purpose. The game itself therefore adds an authentic value to the proceedings.
Two children point to each other and say 'neuf ans' and some children simply say, 'sept' or 'douze'. The teacher circulates as the children get into groups checking they have understood the game:

T: Est-ce qu'il autres personnes, neuf ans. (*The teacher's French although not perfect is understood by the children, and they answer.*)

Ps: Non.

T: Tous les personnes de douze ans? (*To a group of children*) Combien? Cinq personnes? (*The teacher asks each group to verify how many are in their group.*)

P: Non, trois personnes (*A pupil in the group corrects the teacher*).

Driscoll comments:

The children were utterly absorbed in the game. They checked to see that everyone had the 'right' information on their cards, counted the number in their group (in French) and waited eagerly for the next instruction. The fact that the teacher was communicating in French albeit with some mistakes, was unremarkable and taken for granted. The rules of the activity set up an element of spontaneity, so when questioned by the teacher, the pupils had the opportunity to communicate 'for real' when correcting the teacher's assumption about the amount of children in the group. The game of seeking, questioning and finding gave the children a purpose and motivation beyond simply practising the language or pleasing the teacher. For the children the focus of the activity appeared to be firmly rooted in the game. There was evidence of this type of communication very frequently in the lessons in [the 'generalist' LEA] where even the most timid pupils were swept along with the crowd.

There are here examples of good practice in relation to the taxonomy of teaching strategies itemized above as applied to the primary classroom. They are congruent with commonly expressed views of how MFL should be taught at the primary stage. For example, Skender proposes four key features of a primary MFL strategy developed specifically for the teaching of French in Croatia (quoted in Byram, 1999: 145)

1. réparage des éléments de la culture étrangère dans l'environnement des enfants;
2. utilisations des images types;
3. accent sur l'aspect ludique de l'apprentissage à traves les chansons, les jeux, les comptines, les histoires;
4. création d'une atmosphère française.

These four essentials relate directly to what primary teachers seek to achieve in all aspects of the curriculum. They point to the importance of creating a learning environment in which and through which pupils can 'live' a series of structured learning experiences. It can be said that what this amounts to is what was referred to in the previous chapter as the 'primacy of pedagogy' (Sharpe, 1995). Most primary school teachers have always had to teach subjects in which they have no specific accredited expertise. They manage this by applying their reflective understanding of the principles of good practice in primary pedagogy. They draw on a variety of resources to secure aspects of subject knowledge, which as non-specialists they do not automatically possess. In the case of primary MFL there are a range of ways in which this can be done:

● using audio/video/Internet resources to provide native models;
● using foreign language assistants to provide native models;
● using classroom visitors to model the language;
● developing their own linguistic competence.

Most of the models for introducing primary MFL employed by LEAs and clusters of schools provide for these kinds of support in one way or another. Whilst in a transition stage this may involve a secondary specialist taking charge of lessons, eventually there will always be a need for the primary class teacher to 'grow into' full responsibility for effective delivery of the subject in accordance with the principles of good teaching.

The role of games in primary MFL teaching

The use of games, game activities and game contexts is a central tenet of good language teaching at all levels but particularly at the primary stage, where once again we are dealing with engaging situations which make 'human sense' to primary pupils. There are a number of reasons why this should be so, and these are discussed below:

● **Games are enjoyable and promote learning.** Prime among the reasons for using games in primary MFL is simply that games are fun. By playing games in the foreign language there develops a subtle identification in the pupil's mind of the pleasure, excitement and enjoyment of the game with the learning of the foreign language. It is common to find that children who have been taught a game in French lessons will play that game at playtime still in French. Such enjoyment promotes additional practice of this kind and fosters high levels of motivation to learn more. This has to be counted a pedagogic success. Learning a foreign language is actually intrinsically difficult and daunting. Inspiring learners to view the process positively is an important achievement.
● **Games create helpful frameworks for further learning.** A single game format can be used in a variety of language learning situations.

Many games have an inherently 'content-free', 'generic' character which allows them to be adapted to a range of learning objectives. Young children especially like what is familiar, and a game employed by the teacher to promote the learning of one set of structures and vocabulary can often be used to teach others subsequently. The term 'generalisable game activity' (Sharpe and Rumley, 1993; Rumley and Sharpe, 2000) has been coined to highlight this helpful character of well-known games, such as dominoes, bingo, battleships, blockbusters, Chinese whispers, snap, pelmanism, happy families, odd one out, Kim's game, noughts and crosses, etc, all of which provide contexts for teachers to foster knowledge and skills development in relation to almost any substantive linguistic content, at almost any level. For example, even at sixth-form level, a simple game like noughts and crosses can be made highly linguistically challenging by making identification of the square the player wishes to occupy with a nought or a cross dependent on a specified difficult task such as a Molière dictation extract or explaining in French what a constitutional monarchy is. At primary level the same level of pupil challenge can be achieved by putting numbers or picture-icons of places in town in the squares. For more ideas see the above references.

- **Games create situations of real language use.** Games are highly meaningful scenes of interaction for players. Game players develop real intentions, real plans, real strategies and in acting on these the foreign language becomes a necessary resource to be used for real purposes. This provides further direct personal experience for pupils of the normality of the foreign language, helping them to move away from the *idée fixe* that only the mother tongue is for real. Games are arguably the second language (L2) learning situation which comes closest to emulating the conditions of first language (L1) acquisition.
- **Games engage the whole attention of the learner.** The reality of the game demands the full personal engagement of the learner. Games generate hopes, fears, excitement, joy, disappointment. In this way games draw upon the whole personality of the pupil in a way that disembodied exercises to practise the same linguistic point rarely do.
- **Games facilitate necessary repetition of language**. In order to learn a language it is necessary to repeat structures and vocabulary again and again. In itself repetition is inherently boring and tedious. Many of the MFL courses designed in the 1960s and 1970s contained tape-recorded decontextualized structured drills which, really rather unsurprisingly, proved a 'real turn-off' for many pupils. Yet it is true that without a lot of repetition the foreign language cannot be properly assimilated. In the context of a game, however, the tediousness of endless repetition can be

transformed into the adrenaline-fuelled excitement of creating winners and losers, of seeing hopes fulfilled or dashed, of experiencing the exquisite delight of success.

● **Games develop interactive competence, confidence and fluency.** During game activities pupils and teachers have to concentrate on interacting with each other communicatively and efficiently. Because the language required to play the game is always to some extent constrained within defined parameters it is possible for sustained sequences of exchange to develop in which pupils grow in interactive competence, confidence and fluency.

All sorts of games, invented as well as traditional and established games, can be used in all sorts of ways for all sorts of pedagogic purposes. It is possible to deploy them in all of the eight teaching strategies outlined above. They can be taught in the first instance as a whole class activity and then devolved down to group work and pair work; they can be used for teaching new material, for reinforcement or for revision. It is also important for teachers to be constantly alive to the assessment opportunities games provide for evaluating pupil performance and collecting evidence of developing linguistic knowledge, skill and understanding. This point will be developed in Chapter 9.

The role of songs in primary MFL teaching

Much that has been said above about the importance of games and game activities applies also to songs. These too provide the occasion of real language use in a situation perceived as fun and enjoyable. Young children readily imitate sounds, and will usually have learnt to associate singing and playing with rhythms and rhymes with pleasure from an early age. Like games, songs have a strong social function, and 'joining in' with a fun group activity like this reinforces positive attitudes to the foreign language. For primary pupils there is also something 'grown up', impressive and therefore attractive in being able to sing in a language other than one's mother tongue. Through singing traditional songs, made-up songs, catches and rounds, and other age-appropriate material, pupils gradually internalize the structures and patterns of the foreign language as well as the specific language items which the teacher may wish them to learn. Once again the repetition of language, for example in returning choruses or 'cumulative' songs, is experienced as positively pleasurable rather than negatively boring. Singing is a vital part of the life of a young child, inside and outside school, and incorporating the foreign language into this fundamental activity is another way of normalizing it. There are now many commercially available songs suitable for use in the primary MFL class-room in both sheet music and recorded sound formats. The references cited earlier contain abundant examples.

The importance of systematic teaching

The success of games and songs in primary MFL teaching, however, always depends on the teacher's pedagogic expertise and on deep personalized rela-tionships of trust between teacher and pupil. Such pedagogic expertise and trust can be found in primary classrooms among MFL teachers of all kinds, specialists and generalists. The primary generalist does though have the advan-tages outlined in Chapter 6 of establishing both expertise and trust. In partic-ular the primary generalist also has access to the children throughout the rest of the time when they are not specifically being taught MFL. She is therefore in a position to ensure effective integration and embedding of the foreign language, as well as providing the systematic teaching which is necessary if real linguistic progress is to be made. It is useful to view good primary MFL teaching thus as having three elements:

- **Integrating MFL in the whole curriculum.** Ways of integrating MFL in the whole curriculum were explored in Chapter 3. Clearly music and physical education offer specific opportunities for MFL songs and games, but equally number songs and number games in mathematics, or tradi-tional French songs and games in history are further examples of this kind of integration. For the committed and enthusiastic primary generalist MFL teacher a simple song such as *Sur le pont d'Avignon* can be exploited in a range of curriculum areas.
- **Embedding MFL in everyday school and classroom life.** While integrating is essentially a curriculum issue, embedding is much more a 'whole life' issue. In Chapter 1 and throughout this book the value of making the foreign language a part of the child's total school experience has been repeatedly stressed. In addition to the routines and everyday events discussed earlier, teachers often sing with their classes and play games of all sorts: word games, number games, general knowledge games and so forth.
- **Systematic teaching of MFL in planned sequences of lessons.** Systematic and structured lessons are the core of effective primary MFL provision. Principles of good primary MFL teaching can be summarized using that well worn primary device, the acrostic, using the letters of the phrase **Primary MFLs**, as follows:

P   Planning

Systematic teaching of primary MFL needs to be planned at three levels: long-term across the school, medium-term over the class's year, and short-term over the weeks and individual lessons of the timetable. It is vital to provide for continuity and progression in pupils' experience of the foreign language, a point developed further in Chapter 9. At each level aims and objectives should be clear. At the level of weekly and daily lessons there should be defined, delimited objectives for new language items to be introduced.

R   Reinforcement

Reinforcement and consolidation of structures and vocabulary already taught needs to be rigorous and regular. In particular, teachers should seek to use known language in different contexts to maximize pupils' capacity to use the language flexibly.

I   ICT

Teachers should make effective use of all the opportunities now available through ICT to present authentic language and culture to pupils and to assist the process of learning. ICT in its broadest sense is vital to primary generalist teachers without advanced subject knowledge.

M   Modelling

It is vital that pupils are presented with good linguistic role modelling. Again this is particularly an issue for primary generalists, who need to make effective use of real life and electronically delivered native speakers to support their own use of the foreign languages with pupils.

A   Assessment

In order to be certain that what was taught has been learnt teachers need to make regular and efficient use of assessment strategies. Assessment is vital in subsequent planning and in ensuring continuity and progression. Systematic assessment underpins good record-keeping and reporting practices. This point is developed further in Chapter 9.

R   Raising standards

The introduction of MFL as a subject in primary school is intended to raise standards of achievement in the subject at a later stage. It is important therefore that pace and vigour are maintained in individual lessons and that high expectations are maintained throughout teaching schemes over time.

Y   Young learners

The particular circumstances of young learners need to be borne in mind by whoever takes on the task of teaching MFL in the primary school. This means all the things that have been said above about real life contextualization and direct engagement through a strong teacher–pupil relationship. It also means responsiveness to pupils and to the subject, adapting approaches in accordance with pupil response and exploiting opportunities for raising language awareness and cultural awareness as they occur.

M Mixture of activities

Any lesson or series of lessons needs to be characterized by variety in content and activity. Judgement is needed as to how long to spend on any one activity: too long and boredom can set in, too short and the learning may be superficial. The concept of 'fitness for purpose' should always be a yardstick for deciding what to do when. While translation into English should be avoided, discretion is needed in deciding at what point to give explanations in English to expedite the learning process.

F Flexibility

Resources and schemes should be used flexibly. Teachers should be discriminating in what they draw on. Mindless following of a published scheme is unlikely to produce good teaching. Teachers need to make any scheme their 'own', and most schemes are probably best used as one resource among many.

L Little and often

The best way to promote pupil progress is through systematic teaching on a 'little and often' basis – 20 minutes every day would be ideal but is not easy always to achieve in practice. Intermittent or sporadic long lessons are not likely to be helpful.

S Sensitivity

Sensitivity to pupil response in primary MFL lessons is vital to the nurturing of confidence and competence. The great advantage of the primary situation is precisely the opportunity it offers for flexibility. Even in the context of increased prescription in literacy and numeracy the contrast with the formally organized and timetabled setting of the secondary context is still significant. Lessons can still be more easily extended or curtailed according to pupil response, and adapted as informal assessment evidence is accumulated by the teacher.

These principles are important whoever does the teaching. As will be seen in the next chapter, the ways in which they are implemented vary enormously, mainly because primary MFL teaching is not subject to statutory regulation and because there has, at least in England, been no tradition of teaching it in primary schools within any kind of consensual framework through which progression and continuity might be assured. At present a situation prevails in which for the most part primary generalist teachers are applying their pedagogic expertise to a new subject and secondary specialist teachers are applying their subject knowledge to a new context. It is unsurprising perhaps that for the time being the picture emerging is one of diversity and some uncertainty.

To these general principles of good primary MFL teaching needs to be added a commitment to four key ideas which teachers of primary MFL need always to bear in mind.

Four key ideas of primary MFL

There are four key ideas which are crucial to the success of primary MFL teaching. They can be summarized as:

- communication;
- culture;
- context;
- confidence.

To explain the significance of these ideas the four words are each analysed below as three propositions. The 12 propositions taken together are intended to constitute a 'manifesto' for good practice in primary MFL teaching (Sharpe, 1992).

Communication

Proposition 1. The overriding purpose of learning any foreign language is to be able to communicate.
Teaching therefore has to be directed towards enabling learners to communicate with native speakers of the target language.

Proposition 2. Priority should be given to oral/aural communication.
Most communication for most people most of the time is oral/aural, and this is where the emphasis should be laid from the early stages of learning onwards. Reading and writing should be introduced gradually and with caution in the early stages, building upon language encountered in speaking and listening.

Proposition 3. Communication is for real.
Full advantage should be taken of the primary situation to teach young chil-

dren that the foreign language is a normal means of human communication. Language taught in lessons should be authentic everyday usage in the target language culture.

Culture

Proposition 4. Teaching a foreign language necessarily implies teaching the culture in which it is embedded.
The foreign language and its environing culture are inextricably interrelated. Children need not only to learn what to say but how to say it, where to say it and when to say it. They need systematically to be introduced to the rules of social interaction by which native speakers govern their relations with each other. They need, for example, to learn the difference in French between *tu* and *vous*, and to know the importance of kissing and daily handshaking, however unnatural these may seem to English sensitivities.

Proposition 5. A corollary of the centrality of culture is that direct translation should be avoided as far as possible.
Children need to learn from direct experience in lessons that 'this is what people say in these circumstances' in the target language and culture rather than being told this is how to translate 'what we say'. 'Ca va?' is not a translation of 'How are you?'. The two expressions perform similar functions in French and English sociolinguistic settings but they are not synonyms. Interestingly, of course, they only perform similarly as questions. 'How are you' cannot be used as the answer to the question in the way that the statement form 'ça va', can. In the same way 'Et avec ça?' uttered by a shop assistant after something has been bought needs to be heard as 'Anything else?' even though this is not what the words mean.

Proposition 6. Effective teaching of the foreign culture 'from the inside' in primary MFL should aim to help children overcome sociocultural stereotypes.
Through learning a foreign language at a young age the child should develop a sense of empathy and understanding with what is initially sensed as different and alien. Primary MFL teaching should seek to liberate children from the tender mercies of parental prejudice and tabloid xenophobia, and save them from equating being human with being British and viewing everything from a presumed British norm. It should contribute significantly to releasing them from the twin myths of monolingualism and monoculturalism.

Context

Proposition 7. The most important methodological strategy for teaching primary MFLs is the use of contexts.
Using a range of resources: flashcards, real objects, pictures, artefacts, rearranged classroom furniture, etc, and employing extravagant gesture, vivid actions and animated facial expression, the teacher communicates to the children the imaginary L2 context and introduces the appropriate language items. Children understand through the context the general meaning of what is being said, follow the teacher's invitation to join in with it, and so gradually assimilate the language using similar interpretive skills to those they developed to acquire their L1 mother tongue. The essence of the process is having the learner 'make sense' of initially unknown sounds by drawing on contextual clues. The huge differences, however, between the L1 and L2 learning situations mean that the primary MFL teacher needs to provide a deliberate and sharp focus on selected linguistic phenomena, and some L1 explanation of the context to assist time-efficient interpretation and expedite sound understanding may be necessary.

Proposition 8. Through practice in contexts pupils can be encouraged to 'make the language their own'.
The primary MFL teacher needs to make use of all of the 'teaching methods' described above to encourage the learners to take possession of the language being taught as a genuine means of expressing themselves and communicating. The English primary classroom is the place par excellence of 'contexts', where historical situations, geographical areas, mathematical processes and the like from all parts of the curriculum world are all 'brought to life' in colourful and tangible form, inviting learner response and participation. A French pâtisserie may be set up in one corner, with simulated cakes and ice cream, and context cards to prompt the increasingly fluent and confident exchange of communicative French between young English children.

Proposition 9. Contexts cover three main phases in language learning: introduction, practice, reinforcement.
Learners are introduced to language-in-context and then gradually gain ownership through practice-in-context. Provided the teacher has successfully motivated interest and enthusiasm, learners will willingly carry these two forward into reinforcement-in-context and in so doing fix the target items in mind and develop a sense of ease with now familiar language. As suggested above, it is difficult to overemphasize the significance of game activities in securing this final stage.

Confidence

Proposition 10. It is a prime responsibility of the primary MFL teacher to foster pupil confidence in handling the L2 being taught.
From the very earliest stages the primary MFL teacher must have a concern that pupils develop a sense of confidence about what they know and an enjoyment in using it. Perhaps more than any other subject, the teaching of a foreign language exposes pupils to the possibility of appearing foolish or ridiculous. Ultimately it is only the quality of the relationship between pupil and teacher, combined with the teacher's pedagogic skill, which can provide reassurance that there is nothing to fear and a good deal of fun and satisfaction to be gained from making progress in the target language. Primary MFL teachers need to use strategies for avoiding public and direct negative feedback which can crush self-esteem, dissolve motivation and build resentment. While repeated and common misconceptions need to be addressed, the main emphasis should be on reinforcing correct language which is publicly recognized and rewarded.

Proposition 11. Teachers need to feel confidence too.
In order to operate effectively primary MFL teachers need to feel confident about their subject knowledge and their pedagogic skill. Ways in which all kinds of teachers can achieve self-assurance were discussed in the previous two chapters. Suffice it here to point out that it is difficult for teachers who lack self-assurance to convey that all-important sense of confidence to pupils.

Proposition 12. Primary MFL teaching should give children a confidence about language learning in general.
The primary teacher of French is also crucially a teacher of language and a teacher of language learning. Now, and increasingly in the future, adults will need to be linguistically and culturally versatile. Children need therefore to acquire from the beginning a feeling of confidence in approaching a new language, developing a generalizable 'can do' approach to languages as well as specific competence in the particular language being taught.

These 12 propositions encapsulate the essentials of good primary MFL teaching. However, good teaching is not possible without effective assessment within a carefully planned structure which provides for progression and continuity. The teacher must know where pupils are going and how they are progressing in order to be certain that actual teaching events are focused on pupil needs. It is to this vital area that we turn next.

9

Linguistic progression and continuity

Progression and continuity across age groups and phases of schooling

In one sense the issue of progression and continuity is right at the heart of the whole question of the MFL primary teaching. All other subjects of the school curriculum are predicated on the assumption of some kind of linear progression across the years of primary and secondary schooling. Whatever teaching approaches are adopted there is always the basic idea that there will be some process of more or less cumulative development in the subject as the pupil moves through the stages of compulsory schooling. Indeed, it was the apparent failure of the 1960s/1970s pilot project to demonstrate continuous progression which ultimately led to its demise, as described earlier. The evidence collected by Clare Burstall and her colleagues at the NFER (Burstall, 1974) apparently showed convincingly that teaching French in the primary school from the age of 8 did not enable pupils to progress better than starting at 11, there was 'no substantial gain in mastery'. Despite all the criticisms of this report discussed in previous chapters its legacy still holds powerful sway. Many professional and lay educators take the view that unless primary MFL does enable additional linguistic progress to be made there is no point in doing it. Once this position is accepted it then becomes a sine qua non that ongoing pupil progression and continuity in teaching need to be carefully provided for and monitored. This is achieved in two important ways. Firstly, it is important to assess, record and report pupil progress so that subsequent teaching can build on a secure understanding of what the learner already knows. Secondly, it is important that teachers plan systematically for linguistic progression across sequences of lessons over time. In the first part of this chapter the general role of assessment is explored. The second part discusses research on how in practice teachers do and do not use assessment data and other evidence to provide for progression and continuity in primary MFL.

Assessment, recording and reporting achievement in primary MFL

Over the past 10 years or so the issue of assessment has come to assume great importance in teaching generally. This is largely due to the increasing pressure for accountability of education systems in all advanced industrial countries. Broadly speaking, politicians in all these countries see raising educational achievement as the key to ensuring economic success and maintaining economic 'competitiveness' in an ever more harshly competitive global market. There has consequently been a trend in all of these education systems towards, on the one hand, a more precise specification of curricular objectives and, on the other, the development of defined procedures for measuring the extent to which these have been achieved. The predominant political concern has been with viewing education as an input–output process whose efficiency can be gauged by assessing whether predetermined outcomes have or have not been attained.

In England and Wales the Education Reform Act of 1988 represented a landmark in this formalizing of accountability. It imposed on all schools a requirement to teach the National Curriculum and it introduced statutory requirements for the assessment of all pupils. It and subsequent legislation tightened the control on schools through two main forms of external scrutiny. These were the development of an educational 'market' with parents as consumers, and the development of regular systematic inspection of all schools.

Since 1994 the rights of parents have been enshrined in a Parents Charter. The old system of catchment areas in which pupils had to go to a school in the area where they lived has been swept aside, and parents are now able in principle to choose which school they wish their children to attend. To assist them in making an informed 'consumer choice' every school is obliged to publish certain information, including examination and assessment results, and the official report on standards within the school produced by inspectors commissioned by Ofsted.

As Pollard and Tann (1997) note, the publication of end of Key Stage test results constitute 'a means of informing parents about the progress of their children and ... a means of comparing school performance, thence informing an educational market, based on choice and diversity.'

The idea is that 'good schools' will attract more pupils, and with them higher levels of per capita funding, and so flourish and grow, while schools with poor results and critical Ofsted reports will lose pupils as parents withdraw them, lose funding and eventually 'wither and die'. More recently the government has introduced high-speed withering and dying procedures for schools designated by Ofsted as failing, whereby they can be taken over by 'hit squads' of special teams of educational managers, and in cases judged to irredeemable, directly closed.

The establishment of an educational market with 'open access' to schools has certainly contributed to the re-emergence of primary modern languages over the past decade. A CILT study in 1995 found that parental pressure was cited as a key factor by many schools which had introduced the subject. Parents generally view the early teaching of foreign languages as giving their children an advantage and are likely, all other things being equal, in deciding between two primary schools where one offers a foreign language and the other does not, to choose the former. Parents in this respect seem to be taking a decidedly common-sense approach to progression and continuity: primary MFL will help their daughter/son to progress further in learning foreign languages. It is, though, important not to overstress this point. The extent to which parents actually operate as purely rational, discriminating consumers making 'customer' decisions on the basis of quality indicators, especially with regard to the choice of primary schools, is debatable. Despite 'open access' the overwhelming majority of primary-age children still attend the school nearest to where they live, and most parents' overriding concern appears to be that their children should be happy and thriving. It is at the secondary stage of schooling that more judicious selecting really occurs, although it is also at this point that some parents discover that selection works both ways and that, in the case of oversubscribed popular schools, it may be the school rather than the parent doing the choosing.

The relationship between assessment and teaching

Teachers in England and Wales have always been engaged in monitoring pupil progress, but since the late 1980s they have been involved in nationally determined systems of assessment implemented by both Conservative and Labour governments. This high profile political support has meant that significant amounts of public funds have been allocated to improving procedures and over the period since the introduction of the National Curriculum and its associated assessment arrangements teachers have lived through a succession of changes and revisions of official requirements. Whilst for some, perhaps many, this has been a difficult and traumatic process, one undeniable positive consequence of so many changes is that there is a raised awareness in the profession as a whole of the inextricable interrelationship between teaching and assessment.

Assessment has always been part of good teaching. Effective teachers have always sought to relate what and how they teach to their understanding of the present abilities and attainments of the pupils in front of them. As Harlen *et al* (1994: 221) suggest, 'it is difficult to conceive of teaching which does not use some information about the intended learners' starting point.' And Wray and Medwell (1991: 195) firmly declare that 'assessment is not an optional extra in teaching, but an essential, integral part of the process.' Assessment is really about any activity undertaken to appraise pupils' performance. Much of this information is gathered by teachers without their even necessarily realizing, as Foden (1993: 152) notes, 'our professional instincts about a child's achievement arise from the accumulation of information both on conscious and intuitive levels'. In other words there are two inescapable realities underpinning the relationship between teaching and assessment: in order to teach anything the teacher has to know something about what the learners already know and can do; and teachers find out what learners know and can do through a variety of means, both explicit and implicit.

It has become conventional to conceive of assessment as falling broadly into five categories.

Summative assessment. This represents a 'summing up', a check at a particular point in time on what has been learnt or achieved. End of Key Stage assessments in the National Curriculum are summative; they indicate 'where the pupil is' in relation to the defined national levels of attainment. Summative assessment procedures are directed towards marking a specific level of achievement. Most examinations are summative; gaining an 'A' level or being awarded a degree amount essentially to a public recognition that a particular standard has been reached. Summative assessment is always referenced. The measurement of achievement it involves must always relate to a given standard of some sort, and these standards are of two main types.

In *criterion-referenced* assessment the standard is a defined level of achievement. The driving test is an example of criterion-referenced assessment: there is a clearly described set of attainments (specific knowledge, eg of the Highway Code, and skill, eg in executing a three-point turn) which assessees are required to demonstrate in order to meet the standard. Each driving test candidate is measured against this set of attainments and either passes or fails. In relation to MFL teaching generally criterion-referenced approaches have become common, with learners and teachers working towards known specified standards and then making summative judgements against those standards at particular points in time. This is discussed further below in relation to the idea of foreign language 'graded objectives' and National Curriculum assessment.

In *norm-referenced* assessment learners are ranked against a norm, usually based on average performance. IQ tests are a good example of norm-referenced testing. Each person's performance in an IQ test is assessed against the average, the norm, of 100. To have an IQ score of 120 is to be of above average intelligence, to have an IQ score of 80 is to be of below average intelligence, at least in theory, depending on whether it is really accepted that intelligence is what IQ tests measure! In a similar way some competitive examinations have been so constructed as to produce a 'normal curve of distribution', with a few examinees scoring very high, a few examinees scoring very low, and the majority spread across average scores. As far as MFL teaching is concerned this approach tends to be less favoured in an era where the emphasis is on inclusion and achievement by all. Nevertheless there are occasions where teachers wish to rank pupils' achievement and testing to produce a range of scores is useful.

Formative assessment is essentially directed towards maximizing the effectiveness of subsequent teaching. It is the process of gauging what the pupil currently knows and can do in order to be able better to promote further progress. Whereas summative assessment involves making a judgement at a particular point in time of the pupil's achievement, formative assessment is really more concerned with taking stock of what pupils now know or can do in order to inform the teacher about what they need to do next. When evidence is gathered specifically for the purposes of formative assessment it is important to consider the uses to which it is put. Often it does not provide a sound basis for summative judgements, for example, 'Assessment information collected formatively by teachers, when summarised, can be unreliable, and is unsuitable for the purposes of accountability or quality control.' (Gipps and Stobart 1993: 98.) Nevertheless ongoing informal checks on pupil understanding can be extremely useful. Teachers of primary MFL, as much as of any other subject, may wish to reassure themselves that pupils have fully understood a particular language item before moving on to something else which requires it. For instance, it is useful to be sure that children have fully learnt numbers to 31 before teaching them language associated with dates or birthdays.

Diagnostic assessment is, as the name implies, any assessment procedure aimed at diagnosing pupil performance. Diagnostic assessment generates a specific classification of areas of strength and weakness on the basis of which a fuller understanding of how the pupil is functioning can be gained. A widespread example is the use of diagnostic reading tests such as the Neale Analysis of Reading Ability, which yields information about a pupil's capacity in relation to a battery of skills and subskills associated with reading. On the basis of the pupil profile generated in this way specific difficulties which the pupil is experiencing can be identified and appropriate remedial action can be planned. For the most part primary MFL teachers are unlikely to be involved in anything so full blown as this. Nevertheless there are times when it is appropriate to gather assessment information about a pupil's performance and scrutinize it for evidence of particular difficulties which inhibit progress or particular strengths which promote it. It is common, for example, for children with literacy difficulties to do very well in inclusive oral and aural interactive foreign language activities but to perform very differently at the point where reading or writing are introduced, even sometimes at very basic levels such as simply copying signs.

Evaluative assessment. The three types of assessment discussed above measure pupil performance. Evaluative assessment measures teacher performance. In evaluative assessment the intention is to discover how well teaching objectives have been realized. It still mainly involves testing pupils' attainments, but the outcome is not so much an overview of pupil learning as a judgement of the effectiveness of teaching. Individual teachers may use evaluative assessment to monitor their own performance. All teachers know that what they think they have taught may not be exactly what they have taught, and there is considerable research to indicate that teachers' perceptions of what happened during lessons may not reflect exactly what happened. If evaluative assessment reveals that lots of pupils appear not to know something, this probably says more about the teacher than about the pupils. In some countries such as France, for example, the equivalent of Key Stage national assessments are specifically designed to be evaluative, to reveal the 'gaps' in pupils' knowledge so that there is a measure of how the education system as a whole is operating. At the level of the class the primary MFL teacher may wish to make an assessment of how well he or she has taught a particular structure, for example 'Qu'est-ce que c'est?… C'est un/une…' and set up a series of activities where children are required to use it so that his or her overall success or failure can be evaluated. Evaluative assessment can also come suddenly, and sometimes sadly, upon the teacher, as when realization dawns that despite what was felt to be systematic teaching the pupils give evidence of having all forgotten some element of the language. The reverse can happen too, of course, when it becomes apparent that unexpectedly they have mostly all understood something. Evaluative assessment of the quality of primary MFL teaching, where it occurs, is of course now also undertaken by Ofsted, which has since the late 1990s included primary MFL in its regular inspections of primary schools. In this way schools which choose to offer it can be given some judgement on the effectiveness of their provision.

Ipsative assessment. In this type of assessment the focus is on the individual pupil. It is a kind of benchmarking based on past performance: before I knew and could do that, now I know and can do this. Ipsative assessment is about measuring pupils' performance against themselves. It involves assessing what level has been reached by comparison with the levels attained in previous assessments. Ipsative assessment can be shared with pupils, although it need not be. It may be that the teacher simply wants to know whether a child really has made the progress against an earlier assessment that perhaps appears to be the case in class. Where it is shared with the pupil there can be immense benefits for pupil motivation. Getting pupils involved in monitoring their own progress is often the spur to greater commitment to actually making that progress. Sharing learning objectives in primary MFL with pupils has proved to be an effective means of engaging enthusiasm and commitment. There are a number of self-evaluation schemes being used by teachers of primary MFL, including the European Languages Portfolio, which is being adopted by more and more primary MFL practitioners. This document is available from CILT (www.cilt.org.uk).

It is of course obvious that these are not actually five distinctly different types of assessment. Any one assessment procedure could yield summative information about pupil achievement, formative indications of what might usefully be taught subsequently, diagnostic analysis of pupil thinking, evaluative measures of teacher effectiveness, and comparative ipsative scores. What really distinguishes the five forms of assessment is the purposes they serve. We now need to explore further the whole question of the balance between teaching and assessment in primary MFL.

Balance between assessment and teaching in primary MFL

Any primary teacher of modern languages will actually be assessing the whole time they are teaching. In asking questions of pupils in the normal business of the lesson they will be stimulating responses which provide a great deal of information about what pupils know and can do. When the teacher asks a pupil a simple questions such as to give his or her name, 'Comment t'appelles-tu?', the manner of the answer reveals a huge amount about what has or has not been learnt. Does the pupil appear to understand what is being asked? Is he or she immediately responsive? Is he or she appropriately engaged in the interaction? Does he or she appear to know how to respond? Is the response strictly correct? Is it fluently uttered? Is the pupil confident? What about the pronunciation – intonation, accent, patterns of stress, etc? Even with a language item as basic as this the teacher is amassing a vast stock of summative, formative, diagnostic, evaluative and ipsative assessment data. Instinctively, good teachers will exploit data of this kind for the various purposes the five forms of assessment serve. They will use it to make well-founded decisions about what the class has learnt, what the class needs to be taught and the particular strengths and weaknesses of individual pupils.

What we are dealing with here is essentially *implicit and informal assessment*, the spontaneous collection of assessment data through the ordinary processes of teaching and learning in the classroom. The issue which needs to be addressed is the extent to which the paraphernalia of *explicit and formal assessment* procedures that are now integral to the primary curriculum should be brought into primary MFL teaching. In considering this question we also need to take into account the two 'Rs' which are so closely associated with assessment, recording and reporting. Assessment is only a tool to be used, it is not something to be done for its own sake as if it were an end in itself. If formal assessment is to be undertaken it will need to be recorded in some way and at some point it will need to be reported. Clearly the whole point of going beyond everyday informal assessment is to collect and record data in a systematic way so that whatever uses they are put to, the accuracy of the information can be relied on. Teachers are only human, and the kind of informal assessment referred to above is essentially impressionistic in character; it is also transient and ephemeral, and the opportunities for misperceptions, misinterpretations and distorted memories are legion. In this sense, while informal assessment may 'work' on a pragmatic basis to guide the teacher in making on-the-spot classroom decisions, it is not of itself a secure basis for reaching judgements which meet the canons of validity and reliability.

Validity and reliability in assessment

Validity and reliability have become key concerns in assessment in primary education over the past 10 years or so. Teachers need to have assessment information about their pupils which they can count on to portray an accurate picture. It is arguable that unless they are sure the information is valid and reliable, they cannot be sure that the teaching decisions they make on the strength of it are the right ones. In essence, validity means being sure that an assessment procedure actually assessed what it was intended to assess, and reliability means being sure that the results of the assessment procedure were not distorted by intervening irrelevancies. A common example of assessment where validity may be compromised is where children cannot demonstrate understanding of concepts in say mathematics or science because they do not have the reading skill to make sense of the question – this may look like a failure in mathematics or science but it is actually nothing of the sort. Similarly, inability to read, recognize or remember shop signs in French or any other foreign language may not indicate that the child does not know what *un tabac* or *une pâtisserie* is, or that he or she is not capable of using the words in role-play conversations or for real in France.

Reliability is often thought to be high where it is likely that if the same procedure were repeated on another occasion the results would be the same. Much depends on the nature of the assessment procedure being used. Where there are lots of factors involved reliability is difficult to control. Assessments involving group activity, for example, such as some of the earlier National Curriculum Standardized Tasks and Tests, may deliver unreliable outcomes because of the 'chemistry of the group' (Foden, 1993), and children's differing interests and motivations (Gipps and Murphy, 1994). These can be compounded by the labelling of children on the basis of appearance, past performance, personal characteristics and the like, which can underpin a 'halo effect' or indeed a 'negative halo effect' in which certain pupils are perceived never to get anything wrong or always to get things wrong. Nevertheless direct observation remains one of the best methods of assessment in terms of the quantity and quality of the information it yields. As Bradley (1996: 59) notes, 'Observing children's actions while they are carrying out a task lets us see how they do it, whether they change their minds about what they are doing, how they test their ideas and how they share them with others; and this provides more information than merely looking at the product of an activity or what has been written about it.'

Teachers assess through the comparison of performance with some kind of standard that provides criteria against which judgements can be made. While it is in principle of course crucially important that the observations of performance are as objective as possible and made from a neutral standpoint without preconception, it is in practice quite difficult to detach oneself altogether from previous experience and one's perception of pupils. Reliability can be enhanced by the process known as triangulation, through which different kinds of evidence gathered from a diverse range of sources can all be seen to be congruent in confirming a judgement about pupil achievement. For example, if a teacher observes a child in the course of a modern language classroom game being able to identify the months of the year, hears the child correctly saying what the date is or when his or her birthday is in a role-play activity, receives a correct answer to a direct teacher–pupil question about months, and then watches accurate recognition of the months in response to a listening comprehension exercise, that teacher can be pretty sure that with so much triangulated evidence that pupil has learnt the months of the year. Triangulation can also be achieved by using foreign language assistants in the class to repeat assessment activities already undertaken by the teacher. We chance here again upon something good teachers have always done – using information from a wide variety of sources in building up a rounded picture of a child's achievements. And in the end it has to be recognized that 'assessing children's learning is an art, not a science' (Sutton, 1991: 48).

Manageability and convenience in assessment

Validity and reliability are the concerns most commonly expressed in the context of assessment and testing. However, from the point of view of the practising teacher, manageability and convenience are of equal importance. All teachers need to be good managers of time and resources. Teachers should constantly be asking subconsciously: 'Is this a good use of my time? Is this a good use of pupils' time?' The main job of any teacher is to teach, and anything which takes scarce time away from this central purpose should be scrutinized rigorously to see if it is really necessary. Assessment procedures can all too easily become cumbersome and time consuming. Where they have been deliberately chosen or devised by the teacher, as against those which are imposed by higher authority, there is a direct professional responsibility involved and they should be subject to a cost–benefit analysis in order to be certain that the benefit they yield in terms of useful information about pupil progress outweighs the cost in terms of the time, effort and disruption to learning involved in implementing them. This last point is particularly important. Testing can be detrimental to learning not only in terms of the time and effort it takes away from the learning process but also in terms of the possible harm that can be done to the motivation and attitudes of the learner. Teachers should use sensitivity and discretion to ensure that testing facilitates rather than discourages learning.

Ideally, assessment should be integrated into normal classroom learning as much as possible to minimize negative impact. In this way teachers can 'kill both birds', teaching and assessment, 'with one stone', and hopefully not kill any pupil interest or motivation at all. This is not to say that there should never be points at which the pupils are confronted with a more formal situation in which their attainments are to be systematically measured. Provided this has been properly prepared beforehand, the additional challenge and associated 'adrenalin rush' can be experienced as positively motivating, and the ultimate success in achievement as highly rewarding. The question at issue is the balance between such formal test events and more covert assessment undertaken in the ordinary course of classroom activities, and this is a matter of professional judgement. A programme of ongoing assessment, both overt and covert, needs to be devised which can be conveniently fitted into the overall scheme of work being taught. It is, however, important always to bear in mind the need to be sure that assessment does actually contribute to enhancing the quality of teaching and learning. There is absolutely nothing to be gained by assessing for its own sake; there is only any point in making assessments which will have some kind of pay-off for the teacher, the pupil or others with a stake in the monitoring of progress. As Shorrocks (1993) reminds us, 'assessment is a tool to be made use of, it is not something to do for its own sake'. And exactly the same point can be made about recording pupil progress and achievement, 'there is no point in creating elaborate schemes of recording if they are not used and used effectively' (Shorrocks, 1993: 175) so anything included in a programme of assessment needs to clearly warrant its place in terms of feeding back into more effective learning subsequently.

Reporting assessments of pupil progress

It is also important to consider the use of assessment information in reporting. It is essential that the annual report to parents be based on solid evidence of achievement which has been recorded throughout the year. Even though there is no statutory requirement to report on progress in primary MFL, many schools who offer it feel it important to do so. Increasingly teachers are being required to write reports on pupils for a host of external agencies concerned with the welfare of children. Again, it is crucially important that any such reports are securely grounded in an accurate evidence base. Schools therefore need to have systems in place for reporting the achievements of pupils from one teacher to another as children move through the primary phase, and for reporting to the receiving secondary school on pupils moving into KS3. This is vital if continuity and progression across a pupil's school career are to be properly ensured. In the case of primary MFL this is particularly vital given that past schemes have foundered precisely on the question of a lack of proper continuity between primary and secondary schools. However, in practice at the moment it is often found that such records are not kept or transferred on to KS3 teachers, and even where they are the extent to which they are used by secondary schools to ensure progression and continuity through differentiation is doubtful. This issue will be discussed later in this chapter.

Pupil self-assessment

Teachers of primary MFL find benefits in involving pupils themselves in the process of monitoring their own progress. This encourages learners to engage directly with their own learning process and to identify with the learning objectives towards which the teacher is striving. As suggested above, done in this way it is a type of ipsative assessment. At both primary and secondary levels it sometimes takes the form of what has been called the 'graded objectives' approach. This is intended to arouse and sustain learner commitment to achieve and progress in relation to a series of staged MFL standards. Pupils monitor their own development of knowledge, skills and understanding and self-assess under their own control against the requirements of Stage 1, Stage 2, etc, as defined by the scheme being used in their classroom. When they feel confident that they can do the things required at a particular stage they elect to be 'tested', and when successful they gain some certification of the level they have achieved. The system works rather like a driving test which people take when they feel 'ready'. It leaves those who succeed with a sense of 'can do' achievement. Describing the development of the 'graded objectives' approach as it developed with secondary pupils in the late 1970s, Jones (1996) comments:

> ... teachers found that their classes became keen to achieve the defined goals. Success was rewarded and documented. Progress was rapid. Tasks were short, defined in advance, and appeared very relevant to the learners who were frequently cast in the role of visitor to the foreign country. Certificates were awarded for different levels of achievement and most defined the language competences which had been successfully demonstrated by the learners. (Quoted in Swarbrick, 1998: 21)

The principle of graded objectives has been incorporated into some primary MFL schemes. An example taken from the Kent scheme, *Pilote*, is given in Figure 9.1.

Graded objectives approaches do constitute a type of 'formal assessment' but their value lies in relation to both teaching and assessment. Their motivational effect is intended to feed back into the teaching–learning process. Their worth as instruments of assessment resides mainly in the information that they give to the teacher about overall cohort progress. Many primary MFL teachers work with schemes that are inherently 'inclusive' in so far as they are designed to enable virtually all children to succeed, and assessment procedures of this type facilitate the tracking of groups and classes through the various stages of the scheme.

It has to be said, however, that for many teachers of primary MFL (and arguably their pupils) much of the delight of the subject arises precisely out of the fact that it is not a compulsory subject, and as such does not have to be formally assessed in the way that is required for core National Curriculum

What can I say in French

	Yes	Not Yet
1. I can say my name		
2. I can count to 12		
3. I can ask someone their name		
4. I can ask someone their age		
5. I can count to 20		
6. I can count to 31		
7. I can say the month		
8. I can say the day		
9. I can say today's date		
10. I can say when my birthday is		
11. I can say how many brothers I have		
12. I can say how many sisters I have		
13. I can say what pets I have		
14. I can say where I live		
15. I can ask someone where they live		
16. I can ask someone if they have any brothers		
17. I can ask someone if they have any sisters		
18. I can ask someone if they have any pets		
19. I can wish someone Happy Christmas		
20. I can wish someone Happy New Year		

Pupil comment:

Signed:

Teacher comment:

Signed:

Figure 9.1   Example of graded objectives in the Pilote scheme

subjects. The emphasis is on making learning fun. Formal assessment can sometimes be perceived by primary teachers of MFL as inhibiting this, by introducing an atmosphere of threat and possible failure which cloud an otherwise joyous experience. There is, however, something of a contradiction in this position in so far as these same teachers tend to be strong advocates of the value of primary MFL. At some point the value of MFL provision in the primary school has to be judged in terms of the contribution it makes to raising overall standards of achievement in MFL. Without accurate, valid and reliable assessment it will not be possible to argue or refute the case. The likelihood is in any case that sometime in the first decade of the new millennium the non-statutory character of the guidelines contained in the Year 2000 National Curriculum will metamorphose into statutory programmes of study with associated attainment targets against which pupils will have to be assessed. It is important therefore to be aware of the provisional expectations which in a real sense already apply.

Primary MFL and National Curriculum assessment

It used to be possible to argue that as far as assessment is concerned primary MFL as a subject is the same as all other non-core subjects, even though they had formally required programmes of study and it did not. There are many key stage National Curriculum tests for foundation subjects and no official requirement to test religious education. This position has of course been mightily reinforced by the decision of the secretary of state for education that as from September 1998 primary schools no longer had to follow the programmes of study for any foundation subject. In these circumstances it did really become a question of autonomous professional judgement as to what procedures should be put in place to assess, record and report on pupils' progress in these areas. Here it is up to individual teachers and schools to decide what, when, who and how to assess in order to maximize the efficiency of the teaching–learning process. From many points of view this is indeed a valuable freedom. Where formal external tests exist there is always the possibility of 'teaching to the test', ie not teaching what a professional judgement might indicate is in the real interests of the learner, but focusing rather on what is likely simply to ensure success in the eventual assessment. As the Task Group on Assessment and Testing (TGAT) were at pains to point out in the early stages of National Curriculum planning, '... promoting children's learning is the principal aim of schools. Assessment lies at the heart of this process' but 'the assessment process should not determine what is to be taught and learned. It should be the servant, not the master, of the curriculum' (TGAT, 1988).

For primary teachers of modern foreign languages, therefore, the lack of official prescription was arguably something that could be turned to advantage. However, at a stroke, the publication of the KS2 guidelines in the Year 2000 National Curriculum brought primary MFL out of the shadows in relation to both programmes of study and attainment targets to be assessed.

Assessment in the National Curriculum takes two forms: teacher assessment and end of Key Stage testing. Both forms used to apply to all primary subjects, but now apply only to the core subjects of English, mathematics and science. It is envisaged therefore that schools using the National Curriculum guidelines for primary MFL will only be involved in teacher assessment using the 'best fit' approach to locate each pupil at a level in relation to each of the four attainment targets (ATs):

- AT1. Listening and responding;
- AT2. Speaking;
- AT3. Reading and responding;
- AT4. Writing.

Just as the programmes of study discussed in Chapter 4 did not specify substantive linguistic content, no more do the attainment targets which are based essentially on stages of development, as summarized below:

- AT1. Pupils show that they understand:
  - Level 1: simple classroom commands, short statements and questions;
  - Level 2: familiar statements and questions;
  - Level 3: short passages made up of familiar language;
  - Level 4: longer passages made up of familiar language in simple sentences.
- AT2 Pupils:
  - Level 1: respond briefly with single words or short phrases to what they see and hear;
  - Level 2: give short simple responses to what they see and hear (people, places, objects);
  - Level 3: take part in brief prepared tasks of at least two or three exchanges;
  - Level 4: take part in simple structured conversations of at least three or four exchanges.
- AT3 Pupils show that they understand:
  - Level 1: single words in a familiar context;
  - Level 2: short phrases in a familiar context;

- Level 3 short texts and dialogues made up of familiar language;
- Level 4 short stories and factual texts.
- AT4 Pupils:
  - Level 1: copy single familiar words correctly;
  - Level 2: copy familiar short phrases correctly;
  - Level 3: write two or three short sentences on familiar topics;
  - Level 4: write individual paragraphs of three or four simple sentences.

These are essentially the same levelled statements of attainment used for KS3 teacher assessment. In presenting the ATs in this way the document fulfils the hope of the original National Curriculum Working Party on MFL that Levels 1–3 would at some time in the future be covered in the primary years. Interestingly they meant Levels 1–3 of a 10-level structure, whereas now we are being given Levels 1–4 of an 8-level structure. Whether this represents raised expectations nationally is unclear. If it does, there will need to be raised levels of resourcing in their wake. Without substantial investment in focused MFL teacher training there will be little point in having high expectations for all children on an inclusive basis, as discussed in Chapter 6. It is also interesting to note that the attainment targets are 'included to inform planning', which sounds like a 180-degree turn on the position taken more than a decade ago by TGAT, as cited above.

The feasibility of these statements of attainment for primary MFL is of course untested. Taking each attainment target separately, the progression from fundamentals through increasing complexity seems uncontentious. There is always the inherent problem of what exactly is meant by particular terms and phrases, and clear borderlines between levels are always elusive. How many single words or short phrases have to be understood to achieve a particular level? How well does the pupil have to perform in relation to fluency, accuracy, intonation, stress, etc, to achieve a particular level? In the end all of this comes down to professional judgement. In speaking (AT2) and writing (AT4) there is the concrete problem of 'at least two or three' and 'at least three or four' constituting an ambiguity over 'three'. More serious, though, is the less explicit implication that progress might be expected to be parallel in four skills. The issue of the place of reading, and even more contro-versially the place of writing was discussed in Chapters 3 and 4. For many advocates of primary MFL, aiming for a majority profile in which high levels are reached in AT1 and AT2 but where little specific teaching is directed to AT3 and AT4 may appear to be more appropriate than trying to keep progress uniform in all four aspects. Their argument would be that progress in AT3 and AT4 could become rapid during KS3 and KS4 as overall skills of literacy approach those of adults. In other words, assessments at ages 14 and 16 may be unaffected by whether MFL reading and writing are taught significantly in primary schools.

Even though all of this remains non-statutory, it is likely that schools electing to teach primary MFL will increasingly come to plan, teach, evaluate, assess, record and report in the subject with reference to this officially documented structured progression. This has to be seen as a positive development which begins to introduce an element of consistency into what was emerging as a chaotic and uncoordinated area of schooling provision. Eventually it is to be hoped that there will be some exemplification materials to help teachers make best, fit judgements about levels of pupil performance so as to ensure that where AT levels are used as the basis for liaison, continuity and progression between KS2 and KS3, there is some uniformity of view as to what each implies.

It is possible, of course, that having made an exception of MFL once, the government may now be willing to make it an exception again and develop end of Key Stage tests. There are arguments in favour of this relating to the above and to well-known difficulties in teacher assessment as the sole measure of pupil performance. If the subject really is moving to the top of the agenda because of its perceived importance in improving the nation's economic standing and competitiveness, it could well be that it moves alongside numeracy and literacy as something too important to be left as an option or even as an unenforced foundation subject. Advocates of primary MFL should be pleased if it is given such prominence, although anxiety will be felt over the format of any national testing and the effect this might have on both teacher and pupil motivation. In the absence of any such developments for the present, National Curriculum assessment per se does not therefore itself constitute an assessment mechanism, and teachers still need to take responsibility for monitoring and measuring pupil progress in primary MFL. Assessing, recording and reporting performance ('A, R and R', as it has come to be known) in primary MFL involves a number of key principles.

Assessing, recording and reporting – key principles

The key principles involved in assessing, recording and reporting can be summarized by considering three simple questions: Why? What? How?

● *Why undertake the proposed assessment activity?*
There needs to be some clear purpose related to the five forms of assessment discussed earlier. If a clear purpose cannot be articulated, the likelihood is that the time would be better spent teaching rather than assessing. Perhaps the maxim should be 'if in doubt, don't'.

- *What is it that is to be assessed?*
  Assessment needs to have a clear focus on areas of knowledge, skill and understanding related to the intended purpose. Teachers need to be certain that what they are assessing will actually produce information about what they want to find out. It is all too easy to find that the activity undertaken did not reveal what it was intended to reveal. Is a given listening comprehension test activity designed to test word recognition, ability to assimilate gist, understanding of detail, ability to respond appropriately or some other aspect of pupil performance? It is useful to bear in mind the WYTIWYG principle, ie what you test is what you get. It may not always be quite what you wanted.

- *How is it to be assessed, recorded and reported?*
  We need to reflect carefully on the strategy selected and the context in which the assessment is to take place. This latter aspect is of course the reason why so much emphasis is put on assessing in the ordinary situation of classroom activities where pupil performance can be directly naturally observed and measured. Decisions need to be made about the type of assessment, as discussed before, and the form in which it is to be recorded and reported. Listening comprehension can be assessed, for example, in a number of different ways. There may be times when the teacher wants to arrive at a quantitative judgement and sets a formal test with, say, 10 questions with right/wrong answers based on a short taped passage pupils hear twice. Scores out of 10 can then be calculated. On other occasions the concern may be more with assessing pupil ability to listen for the gist of what is being said, and observational comments may be more appropriate.

- *Why record and report this assessment?*
  There is little to be gained from formally recording anything unless it will in some way contribute to enhancing the teaching–learning process. As Kyriacou (1991: 120) reminds us: 'It is important to recognise that the usefulness of keeping records is dependent on the extent to which the records are in fact used. Keeping records that are much too detailed or in a form that serves little purpose will not be a good use of your time.' Such enhancement includes of course writing reports, as well as directly informing subsequent lesson planning.

- *What should be recorded and reported?*
  Test scores are commonly recorded but need to be interpreted for the formative, summative and diagnostic information that they yield, on the basis of which future teaching action can be planned. Observational comments may be logged, but it is necessary to think how these will be drawn on in future lessons and in subsequent reporting. In any event these should be sharply focused and concise and should not be too time

consuming. There is no doubt that however well a teacher knows his or her pupils, the accumulation of observations recorded over a period of time provides a sound basis for reliable reports to be written for parents, colleagues teaching the class subsequently, or a range of other education-related professionals. On the other hand, primary teachers are already involved in a great deal of record-keeping in the core and foundation subjects, and for some primary MFL may be an area where they feel ongoing informal assessment is all that is necessary. However, if secondary schools are to be able properly to build upon the work done in the primary years, they will need to be given records and reports of the levels achieved by the end of Y6.

● *How should this be recorded and reported?*
The recording should be as time efficient as possible and easily accessible afterwards. Writing reports is the same as writing anything: they need to be matched to the intended purpose and audience. All reports should be based on sound and secure evidence, including written records stored as an ongoing process. Reports to parents should be clearly expressed in plain English, reports to facilitate progression and continuity should high-light strengths and weaknesses using professional terminology, other reports for special purposes need judicious professional thought about for whom and why they are being written. With the advent of the 2000 National Curriculum and the non-statutory statements and levels of attainment in primary MFL, reports should indicate the pupil's level in relation to the four attainment targets on the best-fit model discussed earlier.

The most important principle, however, remains that pupils need good interactive MFL teaching, and assessment is only a subsidiary supportive activity. Not all teaching needs to be assessed, not all assessments need to be recorded, not all records need to be reported. A, R and R is important but only in so far as it contributes to pupil progress in MFL learning. Arguably any eventual judgement of the overall effectiveness of primary MFL will be made on the basis of an assessment of its role in promoting pupil progress and raising standards of achievement in the subject. The evidence to date, however, of current practice suggests that in actual primary classroom situations teachers are prioritizing teaching and giving little time to assessment or considerations of transition to KS3.

Planning for progression and continuity

This section deals specifically with current practice in England. A strikingly wide spectrum of different approaches towards continuity and progression appears to be taken by teachers involved in primary MFL. This was clearly apparent in the evaluation of the 18 regional schemes involved in the national Good Practice Project referred to in earlier chapters and by Sharpe (2000). At one extreme, some schemes appeared to give little attention to progression within the primary years and progression across KS2/KS3 broadly on the grounds that what they are doing is a valuable educational experience in itself. In other words, specific detailed monitoring of pupil progress and continuity in provision is not seen as a high priority because of the intrinsic nature of the benefits pupils gained from the experience. At the other extreme, some projects had detailed and structured progression built in throughout and systematic cross-phase links in place. The main stated purpose of one regional project was, for example, 'to secure progression towards a common point of entry at the secondary transition stage'.

Much depended on the nature of the project. Language colleges are 'contractually' committed to work with primary schools and this tends to lead to clearly established procedures for relating the work done in primary classrooms to subsequent MFL learning at secondary level. Such arrangements can give rise to fruitful and mutually advantageous partnerships with good reporting and secondary transition arrangements for pupils. The Good Practice Project contained a number of good examples of how this can be done well with primary pupils' MFL learning driven by human and physical resources supplied and controlled by the secondary school. Whether language colleges or not, it did seem that wherever secondary schools were directly involved in planning and operating projects the issues of progression and continuity through reporting and liaison activities were given a high priority. In some cases this is provided for by secondary staff teaching pupils in primary schools whom they will subsequently teach in KS3. Where the 'drivers' of a project are located in primary schools or LEAs, securing sound progression across KS2/KS3 seemed to involve more taxing challenges.

Assessing achievement, attitudes, motivation, confidence

Among many teachers involved in the Good Practice Project there appeared to be a strong and widespread feeling that formal assessment should be avoided as far as possible. Some think that this is unnecessary and likely to rob the activity of its 'fun' element. Without exception informants reported that MFL lessons are popular with primary-age pupils, and it is clear that eliciting the motivation of pupils is an important principle underpinning course planning, in terms of both content and method. It also appeared to be a widespread view among project participants that SEN pupils respond particularly positively to primary MFL largely because of the emphasis on speaking and listening in the context of activities in which they can succeed. It this sense many teachers believe it gives a second chance to junior age SEN pupils and contributes in this way to the inclusion agenda. In some instances secondary teachers visiting primary classrooms gained impressions of pupil abilities which the primary class teacher found surprising because children who had always had difficulties with reading and writing were able to perform well in oral French or German. Some teachers felt that experiences of success in MFL boosted such pupils' motivation and confidence, and that this had a beneficial effect in other areas of the curriculum. The fact that primary pupils positively like learning a foreign language is an important finding given the well-documented difficulties of engaging pupil motivation in the secondary phase, where it is clear that on the whole they do not. Linked with the enjoyment factor are the high levels of pupil confidence observed by evaluators and related by teachers, headteachers and advisors. In response to questions about whether this could or should be assessed, recorded and reported there was evidence of uncertainty about what the purposes of assessment in primary MFL might be, with typical questions being 'What is it for? Who is it for?' A common view expressed was that it was enough for secondary schools to know in general what 'content' has been covered by cohorts of pupils. Some teachers put forward the view that progression into KS3 essentially consists in secondary teachers' introducing reading and writing after the oral emphasis of the primary years.

There was also a widespread view that primary MFL should not become another arena for individual tick boxes. Whilst there was recognition of the usefulness of ipsative assessments in the form of pupil 'can do' statements, there was a definite reluctance among teachers to engage in formal recording themselves. To some extent this arises from a conception of primary MFL as an enjoyable activity 'outside' the main business of the statutory curriculum, and there was a concern to avoid practices which might risk demotivating pupils. Some teachers contended that apart from using time up it is actually difficult to make assessments of pupils in so little teaching time; in the present circumstances it was felt that there may not be a great deal of differentiating evidence for each pupil individually. Formal assessment and recording appeared less important in closely knit project teams made up of primary and secondary staff, sometimes supported by LEA personnel, who work well together in the context of mutual understanding across age groups and phases. In this sense, close liaison provided an alternative mechanism for ensuring effective progression and continuity. This was especially true where the majority of participating feeder primaries send pupils on to the same receiving secondary school.

Another frequently expressed view was that there is so little time for teaching primary MFL that precious time should not be used up on assessment and recording activities. Many project participants stressed how pressured they believed the primary curriculum to be, and in this perspective it follows that what little time can be found for MFL should be devoted to teaching. Some thought that too much was being made of the issue of progression and continuity. They argued that in practice teachers are intuitively providing for progression all the time in their ongoing interactions with pupils. 'You should be revisiting, testing the water, moving on, extending it, building up the language,' commented one secondary teacher working in primary classes. Others talked of formative assessment being carried on informally without the need for written recording.

Many informants spoke repeatedly of the value of pupil self-assessment backed by teacher comments, and an increasing number of local projects are using the European Languages Portfolio, and adapting it to their local needs circumstances. Some parts of it are perceived to be more relevant than others. In relation to pupils' language experience during European holidays one informant noted that 'most of them go to Florida for their holidays'. However, teachers using the languages portfolio spoke positively of its usefulness as an instrument for cross-phase communication and for motivating children's interest in their own progression, and the importance of giving pupils a sense of progress and achievement appeared to be widely recognized. Several projects have introduced certification/accreditation of pupil achievement to celebrate pupil achievement and motivate future learning.

Secondary teachers in some projects claimed that they can do more as a result of what has been learned in the primary school. In one project, for example, the receiving secondary school is now teaching two languages between Y7 and Y9. For the present though there is little hard evidence of real gains in pupil progress and achievement at GCSE level as a result of primary MFL teaching even in projects which have been running for some years. Teachers in some projects said they proposed to track some pupils. Case studies such as these would be interesting, but a larger scale longitudinal study would be very valuable.

Course/curriculum planning for continuity

It was found that all projects have adopted a systematic approach to planning curricular provision. There appeared to be a broad consensus on general issues in the curriculum provided, with such topics as personal identity, the family, and asking directions being near universal. There was widespread awareness of the QCA guidelines for KS2, although considerable variation in the extent to which they are adopted. Some concerns were expressed about what is perceived to be their 'secondary' character. There was a widely held view that the KS2 MFL curriculum should be distinctive and different from the KS3 curriculum. Primary MFL is seen as something other than KS3 programmes taught to younger children. There is a broad consensus on the fundamental objective of teaching MFLs in the early years, summarized by one teacher as 'Have fun – communicate orally'. Even those projects which do teach reading and writing are still very much grounded in oral work. The principle of little and often was also commonly described as an ideal in planning for progression.

There is, however, great diversity of views on the crucial question behind any curriculum planning in this area. Teachers in the Good Practice Project had differing ideas about why MFL should be taught to primary-age children. The actual activities teachers and pupils within the projects are involved in therefore differed, in some instances quite substantially. Some projects stressed the importance of primary lessons in improving standards of MFL achievement post-11, while others placed the emphasis on creating positive social attitudes, valuing cultural diversity, and promoting tolerance. One project focused on using language for improving international relationships. There is also a contrast between adopting a single-minded focus on language acquisition and a more diffuse notion of learning something of a foreign language but mainly learning to enjoy the process of language learning for its own sake. One deputy head teacher in a project school said she aimed to produce children who leave the school 'with a love of languages'. Similarly, some projects were clearly seeking to teach a language, while others were more concerned with teaching language awareness. Some projects were fundamentally centred on improving multicultural harmony in their areas and more generally combating xenophobia, 'opening children up to experience of the foreign', as one teacher commented. One project coordinator was unequivocal, 'I don't want them to be tolerant, I want them to be positive'. Some projects took a more overtly 'language taster' approach, with one aiming 'to broaden linguistic horizons, celebrate the value of linguistic diversity and provide access to native speakers with a "non-eurocentric" approach'. There is often a link with European dimension objectives. One primary school reported with pride that every member of its staff has visited another European country.

It is possible to classify these differing intentions in the following way:

- language acquisition;
- language sensitization;
- language awareness;
- attitudes to language learning;
- attitudes to European awareness;
- attitudes to multiculturalism;
- intercultural understanding;
- intercultural competence.

In language acquisition there is a single-minded focus on linguistic progress, in language sensitization there is direct experience of a foreign language but less concern with systematic progress, and in language awareness there is a desire to teach children about languages in general. The attitudinal intentions are self-explanatory. The intercultural intentions are distinguished by developing empathy and sensitivity on the one hand or actual skill in foreign cultural situations on the other. The 18 projects involved in the Good Practice Project all differed in the extent to which they believed these intentions to be important. It is reasonable to suppose that all of the schools and projects currently operating outside the Good Practice Project also differ. This constitutes a formidable challenge to any serious planning of curriculum continuity across the primary and secondary phases of schooling.

Contrasting approaches

This diversity in aims and objectives produced some contrasting perspectives on appropriate methods for teaching primary MFL. And all of this directly affects how progression and continuity are conceived and implemented. In the Good Practice Project it was found that conflicting answers were given to fundamental methodological questions such as:

- Should code switching – mixing foreign language elements in with English – be allowed/encouraged/forbidden?
- When should the written form of MFL elements be introduced to pupils?
- How much MFL reading or writing should there be in the primary phase?
- Should rote learning of vocabulary be encouraged/forbidden?
- Should grammatical analysis of MFL structures be encouraged/discouraged? (Some teachers endeavoured to use the literacy strategy approach based on 'word/sentence/text levels', while others thought this inappropriate).

- Should primary pupils be taught one language or several?
- What should be the basis of course planning for linguistic progression – topics/functions/structures/skills?

Opposing views on these sorts of principles tended often to go beyond MFL teaching per se and reflect wider debates in education generally. To some extent it is also a question of primary methodology being brought in to a subject area previously outside the primary curriculum and encountering subject specialist methodology which hitherto had not had to deal with young learners. Primary practitioners' emphasis on giving experience and opportunity for oral discussion prior to any written work, and secondary practitioners' emphasis on teaching fluently in the target language are possible examples which were evident in the Good Practice Project evaluation.

Even within broadly agreed aims there can be divergences of view. Projects directly addressing language acquisition, for example, could be seen to take different approaches to course planning. In one project the concern was that teachers must avoid teaching Y7 content to Y6 pupils, so they cut back on vocabulary – '6 usual, 8 possible, 12 absolute maximum words per topic', 'the minimum number of nouns in the maximum number of structures'. Teachers in this project want to avoid Y7 pupils saying 'Done that'. Others took the view that it is confidence-boosting for Y7 children to encounter structures they have learnt in the primary school and used a 'spiral curriculum' approach where material is revisited and understanding is deepened each time.

The time allocation given to primary MFL varied greatly, and the majority of project participants felt whatever they had was not enough. Even in a project dealing with provision in middle schools covering Y7 as well as the primary years, a key participant observed 'We need a much more even approach across schools', and in his own school, which is firmly committed to the teaching of MFL, he reported that 'You have to fight your corner all the time'. There was a strong feeling that the emphasis on literacy and numeracy weighed heavily on education managers at all levels and that against this backcloth primary MFL may be an unnecessary additional burden, limiting what can be done specifically to enhance pupil progress in primary MFL. Teachers and headteachers frequently argued that the main constraint on ambitious course planning in primary MFL was the pressured nature of the current primary curriculum. This was felt most keenly in KS2 and especially in Y6, where schools were concerned about pupil performance in the SATs. Project coordinators based in the secondary sector and in LEAs reported some resistance from primary headteachers on this account and some reluctance, for example, to release key staff to participate in Good Practice Project conferences which contributed to cross-phase understanding.

Many projects stressed the importance of contextualizing their MFL work within international relationships and school links, and this affected both the time allocation and the manner in which the subject was delivered. In the opinion of many informants the best strategy for dealing with curriculum pressure was some kind of integration of MFL within the primary curriculum (possibly through links with literacy) 'not so much as an add-on as an integral part of the curriculum', as one project coordinator suggested. In this connection it is interesting that some informants thought that traditional exchange trips have had their day, and that it is better to visit other countries for a purpose and include the MFL within that, such purposes arising in connection with areas such as sport, music and, increasingly in the future, citizenship.

Primary MFL and the National Literacy Strategy

Some projects deliberately set out to establish links between primary MFL teaching and the national literacy strategy. However, there was a clear range of differing approaches to the relationship between the two, and these are summarized below:

- Such links are thought to be a good way of making MFL relevant to current primary practice.
- Such links are thought to be a good way of getting policy-makers' attention by 'piggy-backing' MFL on a favoured policy within the standards agenda.
- While there are links which can be made, literacy hour pedagogy and communicative MFL pedagogy do not necessarily fit easily together – grammatical analysis/reading before writing/formalized structure, etc.
- Some headteachers/teachers have reservations about the literacy hour and its required methodology and in these cases the 'piggy-backing' can work negatively.

Once again much depended on the kind of primary MFL project participants were seeking to develop, and some projects fitted better with the literacy hour than others. Taking literacy more generally, however, there appeared to be a broad consensus view that learning a foreign language does contribute to a child's literacy awareness.

Primary MFL and ICT

In the area of ICT, projects appeared to be operating at different levels. Some excellent and imaginative use was clearly in evidence in the Good Practice Project schemes. In one project sophisticated use was made of interactive whiteboards, and in several projects e-mailing was a regular and established part of the work. Video-conferencing to facilitate direct interaction with children in other countries proved valuable in some projects but there was less certainty about the value of using the medium for teaching. 'You can't teach through video-conferencing, only practice, reinforce, celebrate; it has a novelty value but that can wear off' warned one project coordinator. In one project children took it in turns to take home a digital camera to take pictures of themselves and their families waking up, cleaning teeth, eating breakfast, etc. The pictures went on the Web site with captions underneath in four languages describing what is happening in the picture and were e-mailed to partner schools in Europe.

The key principle appeared to be that ICT is not automatically in and of itself 'a good thing' but rather, as with all other types of equipment and resourcing, a tool to be used judiciously for the achievement of specific learning objectives. It was interesting also that ICT emerged as the area of least confidence in the questionnaire responses from Good Practice Project (GPP) teachers. Project participants wrote some comments about poor and inappropriate software. One project coordinator commented that 'there are still a lot of teacher personal training needs and access issues'. Another lamented the undeveloped state of provision for primary pupils, 'I've still to find really useful MFL sites that can realistically be used by primary pupils'. There was, however, praise for the value of the NACELL Web site and an awareness of the developmental state of the field of primary MFL generally.

Primary–secondary liaison and the two cultures

It was apparent during the collection of evidence from the GPP project that the 'two cultures' of schooling continue to impact on attempts to establish effective cross-phase liaison. Primary and secondary teachers and headteachers tended to adopt differing attitudes towards a range of issues in the early teaching of modern languages. Broadly speaking there tended to be a greater emphasis among primary staff on the importance of pupils' enjoyment of language learning and the role of MFL learning in promoting development across the primary curriculum, particularly in relation to literacy and multicultural awareness. Among secondary staff there tended to be a sharper focus on subject knowledge and language acquisition. Each of these perspectives tended to be articulated within the different pedagogic approaches characteristic of the two phases, with teachers in each phase expressing characteristic views about the other. There was, for example, some scepticism among secondary teachers and headteachers about 'the primary ethos'. Similarly, there were concerns raised on the part of primaries about how secondary schools do not take sufficient account of the work done in the primary phase. While these comments arose in discussion about MFL, it was commonly suggested that they applied also in other areas of the curriculum.

In some instances it was manifestly clear that that secondary schools are not building upon what primary schools involved in the Good Practice projects are doing. In one of the Good Practice Project summary reports during the year the project manager notes: 'there is little evidence that secondary schools are building on pupils' knowledge, skills and understanding'. In some areas systems are in place but participants still report that they do not always work as intended. In one project which involved middle schools where cross-phase liaison has been officially in place for a number of years one informant still observed that: 'we send them reams of paper which are ignored'. In the Scottish primary MFL pilot (Low *et al* 1993, 1995) it was found that even when teachers from associated secondary schools actually did the teaching in primary classrooms they taught in quite different ways from the way they taught in secondary classrooms, and this perpetuated the sense of discontinuity for pupils.

There is some feeling still on the part of secondaries that it would be better if primaries did not teach MFL. The main reason offered for holding this view is the perceived lack of subject expertise in the primary sector. Equally important, however, is the perceived problem of coping with pupils from different feeder primary schools. It is difficult for secondary schools to make separate arrangements for those pupils who have had previous MFL experience and those who have not. Furthermore, as is abundantly clear from the Good Practice Project evidence, there is significant variation in the kind of MFL experience primary pupils get. There is evidence from the Scottish project and elsewhere that previous primary experience is not valued by secondary teachers and this causes some resentment and frustration for pupils concerned. Some secondary teachers also wish to retain the 'novelty value' of a subject only statutorily required from Y7. At the same time liaison does not seem always much prioritized by primary schools. Even primary MFL projects involving considerable resource investment sometimes continue to operate without any real cross-phase liaison or concern for what happens to the pupils after they leave the primary school. MFL is a subject with no history of primary–secondary continuity and liaison, and all the evidence suggests that building it up will not be easy.

Many informants made specific reference to cross-phase liaison being in its early stages. Virtually none seemed to feel that they had really established a successful system, although there was considerable evidence of commitment to developing procedures to improve progression and continuity in MFL teaching. The obstacles are, however, perceived to be substantial.

There were in the Good Practice Project nevertheless one or two particularly good examples of liaison working well. In one scheme primary and secondary teachers participate in cluster meetings to design the format for pupil records, called 'My Languages Portfolio', which in future all Y6 pupils will take on to the receiving secondary school. Some primary schools are now committed to using the European Languages Portfolio throughout KS2. In a couple of other projects groups of teachers intend to set up research projects to track pupils from the primary school cluster by visiting lessons and interviews. There is a desire to know how attitudes change, how achievement is affected by early learning, and how KS3 teaching seems to be responding, adapting to pupils with prior MFL experience. In some projects secondary teachers also visit primary MFL lessons and primary teachers observe secondary lessons specifically to improve liaison. Where they happen within the context of a jointly organized primary/secondary project the value of cross-phase meetings is felt to be self-evident. In one such project there are regular meetings consisting of the secondary school head of department, the secondary MFL coordinator for KS3, primary teacher representatives from each of seven participating schools (including one headteacher), the LEA MFL advisor, and one link advisor. Members of this team have a real sense of ownership of their project and have made great progress in building efficient cross-phase liaison.

There were in the Good Practice Project also examples of secondary schools making specific provision for pupils who have been taught MFL during the primary phase. A language college is making arrangements for all pupils who have learnt MFL to be taught in a block instead of in the usual 'socially mixed' classes (ie from different feeder primaries). It is hoped that some of the pupils will be fast tracked to GCSE. The expectation is that these pupils will be more confident, less inhibited and make faster progress.

Conclusion

Planning for linguistic continuity and progression on the one hand and assessing, recording and reporting pupil achievement on the other are the two platforms on which a coherent MFL learning experience can be provided for pupils. While the general principles of good practice in both aspects are widely understood and agreed within the teaching profession as a whole, there is considerable evidence of variation in practice based on differing philosophies and methodologies in primary MFL teaching. Divergent practice also arises from the non-statutory position of the subject. At the time of writing there is no certainty as to whether this will change.

Part 5

Future issues

10

Future research, development and policy making

In this chapter we consider a possible agenda for the future development of, and research into, primary MFL. This overview agenda attempts to draw together issues discussed in each of the preceding chapters and to set them in the context of research and policy making in education generally. Specific research in the area of primary MFL is not voluminous given the history of the discipline, and much ongoing policy analysis is therefore informed more by educational philosophies and ideologies than by unequivocal findings from definitive empirical studies. Nevertheless, those in positions of responsibility for education systems around the world all have to find answers to Lenin's famous question: 'What is to be done?', and therefore have to make decisions on the best information available. The following seven key questions taken together would seem to constitute essential agenda items for research and policy making over the next decade.

- At what age should languages be taught?
- How much time should/can be given to primary MFL?
- Which languages should be taught?
- What can be learnt from the experience of other countries?
- How can continuous MFL learning be provided for?
- How should teachers of primary MFL be trained and supported?
- Should MFL become a statutory part of the primary curriculum?

At what age should languages be taught?

Research relating to this issue was discussed in some depth in Chapter 2. While there is some evidence that starting earlier gives some advantages because of the additional time learners then have to make progress in learning a foreign language, there is no clear-cut evidence that merely teaching at a younger age has benefits. Following a comprehensive review of relevant research, Singleton (1989) concluded it simply cannot be assumed that 'younger = better' in the sense of 'better in all circumstances'. Much of the evidence is contradictory and there are important contextual factors always to be borne in mind. Learning a foreign language in school is quite different from learning a language in a naturalistic setting in the home environment. The rapid progress young children make in their mother tongue in the early years cannot per se be used as a basis for believing that they will necessarily learn a foreign language in the classroom easily. Progress will only be made provided there is continuous, systematic and responsive teaching. Mitchell, Martin and Grenfell (1992), for example, comment that 'investment of more hours, through an earlier start, has at least the potential to raise general levels of achievement, provided that issues of continuity and progression are properly addressed'.

There is to date, however, scant evidence on whether an early start really makes a difference to later success in formal assessments (Sharpe and Driscoll, 2000). One case study is that of Scotland, where the MFL project has been in existence long enough to enable comparisons to be made between pupils who had been taught MFL in primary schools and those who had not. Studies undertaken by Low *et al* (1993, 1995) and Johnstone (1997) indicated that:

- Performance at age 16 at Standard Grade appeared to be much the same, at least in average terms, as it had been before the National Pilot began.
- A wider range of pupils than before was reaching Standard Grade, including many who previously would have opted out and not taken a language at Certificate level.
- Almost the full ability range of National Pilot pupils had reached the same average level of performance in the first national examination as the top 40 per cent had formerly achieved.

On the basis of a survey of published research from other European countries Martin (2000) suggests that there is no conclusive evidence yet that early MFL teaching makes a substantial difference to children's attainment at secondary school. She reports that there is some indication in the evidence base that 'any advantage may be limited to certain competencies, typically pronunciation or listening comprehension'.

The position thus is one in which schemes for the introduction of MFLs into the primary curriculum are being implemented in a number of countries on the basis of a general view that this is a good idea but without substantial evidence from research that clear benefits would be gained. However, as Martin notes from the research literature, 'there is evidence that outcomes are positive at the end of primary schooling'. Furthermore, the Scottish evidence quoted above suggests that there may have been an improvement in the attitude of pupils towards MFL and a rise in overall motivation to learn foreign languages. The evaluation of the Good Practice Project also reported very high levels of pupil enthusiasm for and engagement with primary MFL lessons. As time goes on there will be more opportunity to study pupils at the stage of formal examinations who have had primary MFL experience. This will be an important area for future research, with growing implications for future policy making. We really need to be able to be more certain that the suggested benefits from the Scottish experiment in terms of raising overall levels of motivation and achievement are definite and enduring. We also need to know whether they can be generalized south of the border.

How much time should/can be given to primary MFL?

It follows from the above that the amount of time a pupil spends learning a foreign language is a major factor in determining how much progress is made. Again it is important to emphasize that it is not the only factor, but some researchers consider it to be very significant. Edelenbos, for example, felt that 'time for learning' was the only classroom variable which influenced pupils' scores in listening, reading and vocabulary tests (Edelenbos and Johnstone, 1996). Martin (2000) reports research by Genelot in 1996, which showed that in the first phase of the experimental primary MFL project in France the longer the period of 'initiation', the better was the attainment of pupils. Radnai (1996) found that actual classroom hours spent in MFL teaching/learning provided the highest correlation with pupil achievement.

In the English context, however, in 1995 CILT undertook a survey of English primary schools providing a foreign language and found that the time devoted to the subject varied from as little as 10 minutes per week to as much as 120 minutes per week. In some research evidence and in evidence from the Good Practice Project the principle of 'little and often' was strongly adhered to. However, equally clear from the Good Practice Project was the finding that teachers and headteachers felt the primary curriculum was already overloaded and that schools struggled to find time to teach a foreign language. Here too is an important area for future research. As noted many times in previous chapters, there is currently huge diversity in patterns of primary MFL provision in England involving varying time allocations. Charting the correlations between these different approaches to curricular time and pupil performance would yield valuable information for future policy decisions.

Which languages should be taught?

This is currently an area in which pragmatic expediency and rational principle come somewhat into conflict. In England there has been for some time a concern among policy makers that it is a good thing to diversify the range of languages taught in schools. This is mainly because French continues to predominate as the first foreign language in most English schools, while the reasons for its predominance have been rather 'lost in the mists of time'. The claims of Spanish, German and other languages, including Japanese and Chinese, have become much stronger.

Where pupils only begin to learn a foreign language at secondary school diversification can more easily be achieved than where they arrive having already begun to learn a language in the primary school and wish to continue with it. Often this is a parental wish also. In the present unregulated state of primary MFL provision the most common language taught in primary schools is French, largely because this is the language primary teachers are themselves most likely to have learnt as pupils. There is some evidence that the growth of primary French is impacting on the diversification policy in both England and Scotland. While it can be argued that switching languages at age 11 does still give the pupils an advantage over pupils who have studied no language at all in the primary school, it defies common sense to say that there is not some loss of continuity. Nonetheless, some research into the progress made by mixed cohorts of secondary pupils studying, say, German, where some had done German in the primary school, some had done French in the primary school, and some had not studied any language, would be instructive, and would feed directly into the broader diversification agenda.

What can be learnt from the experience of other countries?

Much reference has been made throughout this book to the Scottish national pilot project. A survey carried out between November 1998 and June 1999 found that 76 per cent of schools (1696) taught French, 20 per cent (467) taught German, 1 per cent (30) taught Italian and 2 per cent (49) taught

Spanish. Roughly 11 per cent of Scottish primary schools were teaching two languages. As indicated earlier, the project moved from being based on visiting secondary teachers to a more primary delivery model. The same survey found that 39 per cent of the teachers taught only their own class, 25 per cent taught their own class and other classes, and 36 per cent taught only classes for which they were not the class teacher. It is important, however, to emphasize the extent to which the Scottish experiment has been supported with a significant infrastructural resource including:

- support and advice from HMI;
- a National Committee for the whole project;
- regional steering committees;
- national development officers;
- regional advisors;
- guideline documents;
- newsletters;
- significant levels of resourcing;
- significant levels of language training/staff development.

This was a national project to cover the whole country. In that sense it resembles provision in many other European countries. Commonly pupils on the continent begin to learn a foreign language between the ages of 8 and 10. Primary school teachers in some countries, such as Spain, Greece and Italy, are expected as part of their professional responsibilities to be able to teach a foreign language.

In France a national experiment, *Enseignement Précoce des Langues Vivantes*, was launched in 1989 to teach a foreign language to pupils in the final year of primary schooling. Again this was a national scheme, although in the first instance not intended for all schools, and based on the provision of two 45-minute teaching sessions, provided by visiting secondary language teachers, primary teachers with language competence and other competent adults who might or might not be teachers. In 1992 the experimental phase was completed and it was decided to extend the provision. By 1995, 55 per cent of final-year primary pupils were being taught English, German or Spanish, with English being by far the most widespread. Strict methodological guidelines were provided by the Ministry of Education in Paris. Later the teaching was extended to cover pupils aged seven and eight and the range of languages broadened to include Arabic, Italian and Portuguese. A video was produced to be used in all schools, and by the turn of the century all children aged ten and eleven were being taught. In a recent statement by the minister of education, Jack Lang, it was made clear that the teaching of modern languages in French primary schools was to be given higher priority in coming years.

In Germany there is a similar picture. Most pupils start to learn a foreign language at the age of eight. In Spain and Italy the teaching of primary MFL goes back to the 1970s. In both countries considerable importance is attached to the subject and up to three hours per week is allocated. Similar approaches are taken in The Netherlands, Scandinavia and Greece.

There are signs that this level of activity in primary MFL in other member states of the EU is exerting an influence on the thinking of English politicians and policy makers. In particular the commitment to resourcing a national project in Scotland over the past decade makes a stark contrast with the prevailing policy towards provision in England. There is much to be learned from the experience of these countries (see for example Blondin *et al*, 1998). It is to be expected that whatever decisions are or are not taken by government authorities in England in the short term, there will be ongoing monitoring of the outcomes of primary MFL schemes in a range of countries.

How can continuous MFL learning be provided for?

At various points throughout the discussion in preceding chapters the importance of progression and continuity has been stressed. It might be useful to define these two terms.

Progression: assessment and evaluation of learner performance and achievement in order to promote systematic ongoing improvement.
Continuity: systematic planning of teaching in order to secure effective pupil learning.

These two terms point to the vital role of three processes:

1. Assessing pupil progress.
2. Linguistic planning.
3. Liaison between teachers and schools.

Existing evidence suggests that English primary teachers involved in MFL teaching have reservations about all three of these processes. Some of this was discussed in Chapter 9. The evidence includes findings from the evaluation of the Good Practice Project. Here it was found that primary teachers' attitudes to progression and continuity varied across a spectrum.

Primary teacher attitudes towards progression and continuity in primary MFL

| intrinsic value in itself | _____ | progression towards entry into secondary phase |

At one extreme, teachers took the view that what they were doing was so valuable as a pupil learning experience in its own right it did not matter that it was not being systematically followed up or built upon subsequently in the secondary phase. At the other end of the spectrum, teachers were planning carefully to ensure that their work fed into the secondary curriculum. In most cases teachers advocating the 'intrinsic value' approach gave a high priority to pupils' enjoyment of learning the foreign language, almost to the point of seeing this as an end in itself. In this perspective formal assessment seemed inappropriate. They tended to emphasize the holistic character of primary learning. Given the research findings described earlier, particularly the evidence above about Scottish pupils' performance at 16, which suggest that motivational factors in pupil MFL learning are critical, it may be that this emphasis on enjoyment of language learning at the primary stage is important. Ironically, therefore, it may be that in the end some primary teachers are succeeding in influencing their pupils' subsequent success in the secondary phase by not being too concerned with formal assessment and detailed planning of progression.

The extent to which MFL is a linear or a thematic/modular subject was considered in Chapters 4 and 9. Given the present uncertain state as to exactly what the subject is and what it is for, it is difficult to be too prescriptive about how linguistic planning for continuity should be assured. There can, however, be no such equivocation about the value of liaison between teachers and schools. Whatever the aims and objectives, the scope and curriculum, or the methods and practices in place in any given scheme of primary MFL, it is always helpful to pupil progress for there to exist good communication between successive teachers and between feeder primary and receiver secondary schools. Further research on how this is achieved in different contexts would be extremely helpful. Liaison is costly in terms of teacher time, and finding effective and expedient ways of maximizing the information flow would improve the benefits to pupils moving between teachers and schools.

How should teachers of primary MFL be trained and supported?

A basic analysis of the training needs of different types of primary MFL teacher was presented in Chapter 7. Experience from the GPP indicates clearly that involvement in a supportive cluster of primary and secondary schools, perhaps with LEA support, provides positive support to MFL teachers. Where the teaching is being undertaken by primary generalists, the provision of support by a specialist on site, by a secondary specialist from an associated secondary school or language college, or by LEA personnel also appears to be very important. The most significant training needs of primary generalists are to develop the confidence to tackle the subject, to acquire sufficient elementary knowledge to be able to deliver the substantive content, and to become familiar with the resources through which their teaching can be supported. The present situation in England, as revealed by the GPP, is one in which in some parts of the country primary teachers are being supported in 'having a go' at this subject and gaining in confidence with experience, while in other parts of the country their counterparts have a firmly entrenched conviction that they could never teach a foreign language. In the evaluation of the GPP it was found that even in primary schools where visiting specialists from the receiving secondary school had for many years been delivering MFL lessons, in which the class teachers had always participated, those same class teachers felt they could not do the teaching themselves. The contrast between these different groups of primary teachers was astonishing and highlighted the importance of attitude and self-esteem. We need to know more about how primary teachers' conceptions of their role and what they are able to do can be shaped by training experiences.

Should MFL become a statutory part of the primary curriculum?

Edelenbos and Johnstone (1996) observed that:

> Even in a country such as the Netherlands where the social context for English at primary level is comparatively much more favourable than in many other countries, fourteen years of gradual development were necessary before English became an obligatory subject and eighteen years before official, national core goals were implemented.

This is a sobering thought. It underlines the importance of setting the hopes and desires of advocates of primary MFL in a clearly realistic context. Research evidence commissioned by the QCA in 2001 found that in England only approximately 21 per cent of KS2 primary pupils are being provided with any kind of MFL teaching. Furthermore, there is some evidence that there has been a decline, since pressures on primary schools to fulfil statutory requirements of the National Curriculum and to deliver the literacy and numeracy strategies have increased. The QCA research suggested that despite this decline attitudes towards *the idea* of MFL in the primary curriculum were overwhelmingly positive, and among teacher and headteacher informants there was a broad welcome to the various steps being taken to provide 'official' guidance, particularly the QCA Guidelines and the production of the detailed Scheme of Work for KS2. There is also little doubt that parents think primary MFL is a 'good thing', and this fact often underpins the attitudes of headteachers, who tend to see this as an additional 'marketing' resource. One headteacher caricatured typical parents of his pupils thus: 'Well of course I send my children to School X, they do French there you know...'

Current evidence may point to primary MFL generally being viewed as a 'good thing', but this is matched by a strong feeling that the practicalities of implementation are daunting in present circumstances. There is the famous principle 'Well, I wouldn't start from here'. Unfortunately there is of course no other starting point; we are where we are, and any decision about statutory inclusion has to be made in the prevailing context. It is clear that this context is characterized by the following:

- There is widespread acceptance of the value of teaching MFL to primary-age children.
- The primary curriculum is already heavily loaded.
- Primary schools are under pressure to deliver on high-profile government policy initiatives.
- Many primary teachers and headteachers, probably the majority, do not believe MFL should be a statutory requirement at KS2 or KS1.
- Many secondary teachers and headteachers, probably the majority, do not believe MFL should be a statutory requirement at KS2 or KS1.
- There is wide variation in the attitudes of LEAs towards primary MFL.
- There is a shortage of specialist MFL teachers.
- Primary teacher training does not include MFL in its curriculum.
- Where primary MFL exists currently it does so because of the commitment and enthusiasm of key individuals.
- There is wide variation in what is actually being taught under the heading of primary MFL.

It is unsurprising therefore that the starting point is one in which the subject has a presence only because of the determination and resilience of teachers, headteachers and LEA personnel acting in their own local circumstances. Where the subject survives over time it is usually because an effective team of committed individuals has been formed. A key finding from the evidence gathered in the evaluation of the GPP was the importance of building good teams in successful primary MFL projects. The most positive results appeared to be associated with projects where groups of professionals worked together towards common goals within shared frameworks of understanding and clearly defined roles. In one LEA-led project, for example, many of the advisory service were involved: the ICT advisor, the literacy advisor, the MFL advisor plus staff from the language college and committed primary headteachers and teachers. One teacher wrote in the questionnaire: 'The rest of the staff have to believe in it. They also have to feel confident and convey enthusiasm. These are absolutely vital otherwise the MFL teaching will not succeed.' This comment is undoubtedly a fair summary of how matters stand at the time of writing.

In the light of this analysis the recommendation arising out of the recent Nuffield Languages Inquiry that all children should be taught MFL from the age of seven appears to be something more in the way of a distant hope than an available policy option. However, the interim proposal 'to spearhead the commitment' by funding international primary schools and introducing language awareness into the National Literacy Strategy does seem to open up a way forward and certainly accords with much work already underway in a number of local projects, including those participating in the GPP. This 'interim proposal' sets an agenda to be taken forward by building on the growing strength of existing provision and encouraging further development. The GPP offers a model of how a differentiated agenda can foster valuable development towards a longer-term goal at relatively modest cost and providing sound value for money. As things stand, and taking into account the high-priority government agendas on literacy, numeracy and ICT, it seems sensible to continue to provide support and encouragement to local initiatives. In this way an evolutionary development may be fostered which will change some of the key characteristics listed above and thereby create a more conducive context for making the teaching of MFL in primary schools compulsory.

The Nuffield Languages Enquiry team also emphasized the value of incorporating primary MFL within the key skills agenda for young children, and this view parallels some of the philosophies espoused by primary MFL advocates discussed in previous chapters. 'The need to strengthen our children's literacy, numeracy and technology skills is clear and we support it. Side by side with these should go the ability to communicate across cultures. It too is a key skill.'

This equating of language skill with 'the ability to communicate across cultures' resonates strongly with central ideas in many of the GPP projects, for example. It also highlights once more the current absence of a clear consensus definition of what is involved in teaching primary MFL. Most stakeholders agree that it is not simply a question of transposing KS3 MFL to KS2. The subject is perceived to be distinctly different from secondary MFL. The task ahead is to engage primary educationists and MFL subject specialists in a dialogue about what can and should be taught in the primary phase.

In fact, of course, there is ambivalence among primary MFL enthusiasts about the question of statutory compulsion. They want MFL teaching to be compulsory in order to ensure universal provision and a common pupil entitlement. They also believe that if this happens money and resources will be made available to develop it. However, they do not always warm to the idea of having required programmes of study and formal assessment. As indicated in previous chapters, they tend to value the autonomy they currently enjoy. It is likely that this level of personal commitment and 'ownership' underpins the success of many of the current projects. In this sense it is arguable that the successes and positive attitudes found in existing local projects actually depend upon primary MFL being non-statutory. One headteacher in the GPP noted, 'we own it at a time when we have so many things being imposed'. It is likely that his attitude would be different if it were 'imposed'.

Primary practitioners tend to feel sensitive about the imposition of a top-down approach, which they perceive to a significant extent to be informed by a secondary perspective. Yet they are aware that in terms of pupil attitudes and motivation the success they encounter stands in some contrast to the position in secondary schools, where pupil negativity about MFL is a serious concern. It may not be unreasonable to suggest that while some of the problems at secondary level are due to more general factors such as the position of the English language in the world and the nature of adolescence, some at least may result from the curricular and pedagogic approaches currently characteristic of secondary schooling. One clear implication is that there needs to be dialogue between primary and secondary teachers and that secondary schools need to reconsider what they are doing in MFL at KS3. Primary MFL cannot be divorced from secondary MFL. It needs to be seen as a secondary issue as well. It seems reasonable to argue therefore that nothing should be imposed until this dialogue has taken place.

Ultimately what is required is a continuous policy for the development of pupils' linguistic understanding from the early years through to KS4. This is a huge undertaking and one of great significance for the future. The bottom-up growth of primary MFL shows how educational professionals working together in local settings can build up mutual understanding to create the conditions to raise pupils' achievements and produce useful information about what works and what does not work. Recently a number of strategic policy initiatives in a number of countries have been developed centrally which have not always operated locally in the way their designers intended. There appear prima facie to be strong grounds for adopting a strategy of moving towards a coherent primary/secondary languages policy through supporting and developing local initiatives. Central government has only recently invested any funding at all in primary MFL through the Early Language Learning Initiative, which at the time of writing has been running for 18 months – hardly long enough for real embedding to take place and for complex issues of curriculum and pedagogy to be properly addressed. Much could be gained by extending the initiative within an overall policy of gradualism rather than a 'big bang' approach to making primary MFL a statutory part of the National Curriculum

Afterword

The incoming British government following the June 2001 election is still led by the only prime minister ever to have spoken publicly and positively about primary MFL. Tony Blair and his ministers will need to respond to the recommendations of the QCA working group, submitted earlier in the year. These advocate the value and benefits of an early start to modern language teaching, but express caution about any hasty move towards compulsion and statutory requirements.

In truth, the introduction of statutory regulation is not likely to be on the agenda. The National Curriculum has already been slimmed down to enable schools to concentrate on the core subjects and to give them more freedom to make curricular decisions in their local circumstances. Preference is almost certain to be given to a range of supportive measures, such as the extension of language colleges and further funding for the Early Language Learning Initiative and similar schemes.

There is some equivocation over the role of LEAs. On the one hand, there are good examples of LEAs driving the primary MFL policies forward (Richmond, Kent, Liverpool). On the other hand, LEAs are sometimes seen by governments to be part of the problems rather than the solutions in education. There will probably be more working groups and steering groups to give time for thinking and development. The training of small but growing corps of primary MFL specialists will probably be taken forward, although in its first year the place allocation was undersubscribed. The aim may well be to 'let a thousand flowers bloom' and begin to foster a critical mass that can catalyse the emergence of widespread provision of MFL teaching in primary schools.

Policy makers' eyes are likely also to be on the situation south of the English Channel, where a far-reaching national vision of primary MFL universal provision is being put in place. In France, the development is being articulated in high-flown rhetoric and progressed through the *grandes conceptions* of national politicians, whilst north of the Channel, things move forward uncertainly on the basis of pragmatic localized notions like 'perhaps it would be a good idea to have a go at it'. This is absolutely in keeping with the historic traditions of the education systems of the two countries. It is also entirely appropriate that both countries, and others across the continent, should be making the effort in 2001, the European Year of Languages. In 1901, it would have been inconceivable – in 2001 it looks possible. Maybe in 2101 everyone will wonder why it took so long!

References

Alexander, R (1984) *Primary Teaching*, Holt Rhinehart and Winston, London

Alexander, R, Rose, J and Woodhead, C (1992) *Curriculum Organisation and Classroom Practice in Primary Schools*, Department for Education, London

Ball, S J (1992) *Reforming Education and Changing Schools: Case studies in policy sociology*, Routledge, London

Bell, G H (1989) *Europe in the Primary School: A case study*, Pavic Publications, Sheffield

Blondin, C *et al* (1998) *Foreign Languages in Primary and Pre-school Education: Context and outcomes, a review of recent research within the European Union*, Centre for Information on Language Teaching and Research, London

Bradley, L S (1996) *Children Learning Science*, Nash Pollock Publishing, Oxford

Brumfitt, C (1995) *Language Education in the National Curriculum*, Blackwell Publishers, Oxford

Buckby, M (1976) Is primary French in the balance?, *Modern Language Journal*, **60**, pp 340–46

Burstall, C *et al* (1974) *Primary French in the Balance*, NFER Publishers, Windsor

Byram (1999) *Language Learning in Intercultural Perspective*, Cambridge University Press, Cambridge

Canale, M (1983) From communicative competence to language pedagogy, in *Language and Communication*, eds J C Richards and R Schmidt, Longman, Harlow

Chomsky, N (1965) *Aspects of the Theory of Syntax*, MIT Press, Cambridge, Mass

Dearing, R (1994) The National Curriculum and its Assessment, School Curriculum and Assessment Authority, London

DES (1987) *Modern Foreign Languages to 16*, HMSO, London

DES (1992) *Developing the European Dimension: Some policy models*, HMSO, London

DES/Welsh Office (1990) *Modern Foreign Languages for Ages 11 to 16, Proposals of the Secretary of State for Education and Science and the Secretary of State for Wales, Harris Committee*, HMSO, London

DfEE (1999) *The National Curriculum*, HMSO, London

Donaldson, M (1991) *Children's Minds*, Fontana Press, London

DfEE (1995) *Modern Foreign Languages in the National Curriculum*, HMSO, London

Driscoll, P (1999) Teacher expertise in the primary modern foreign languages classroom, in *The Teaching of Modern Foreign Languages in the Primary School*, eds P Driscoll and D Frost, Routledge, London

Driscoll, P and Frost, D (1999) *The Teaching of Modern Foreign Languages in the Primary School*, Routledge, London

Edelenbos, P and Johnstone, R (eds) (1996) *Researching Languages at Primary School: Some European perspectives*, CILT, London

Escartes-Sarries, V (1990) Onions and stripey tee-shirts, or, how do primary pupils learn about France?, *Journal of Modern Language Teaching*, February

Foden, A (1993) Integrating assessment into the curriculum, in *A Science Teacher's Handbook*, ed R Sherrington, Simon and Schuster, London

Gamble, C J and Smalley, A (1975) Primary French in the balance – 'Were the scales accurate?', *Journal of Modern Languages*, **94** (7), pp 94–97

Giovanazzi, A (1992) Sense or sensibility? *The Organisational Imperatives*, Diddier, Paris

Gipps, C and Murphy, P (1994) *A fair test?: Assessment, achievement and equity*, Open University Press, Buckingham

Gipps, C and Stobart (1993) *Assessment: A teacher's guide to the issues*, Hodder and Stoughton, London, p 98

Harlen, W, *et al* (1994) Assessment and the Improvement of Education in *Teaching and Learning in the Primary School*, eds A Pollard and J Bourne, Routledge, London

Hawkins, E (1984) *Awareness of Language: An introduction*, Cambridge University Press, Cambridge

Hawkins, E (1987) *Modern Languages in the Curriculum*, Cambridge University Press, Cambridge

Hawkins, E (1996) Languages teaching in perspective, in *30 Years of Language Teaching*, ed E Hawkins, CILT, London

Hawkins, E (1999) *Listening to Lorca*, London, CILT

Hoy, P H (1977) *The Early Teaching of Modern Languages: A report on the place of language teaching in primary schools by a Nuffield Foundation Committee*, Nuffield Foundation, London

Hurrell, A (1996) The teacher as traveller: keynote address, in *MLPS in Scotland: Practice and prospects*, proceedings of two conferences on modern languages in primary and early secondary education, ed L Low, Scottish CILT, Stirling

Hurrell, A (1999) The four language skills: the whole works!, in *The Teaching of Modern Foreign Languages in the Primary School*, eds P Driscoll and D Frost, Routledge, London

Johnstone, R (1994) *Teaching Modern Languages at Primary School*, SCRE, Edinburgh

Johnstone, R (1997) *Case Study Notes: Researching primary MFL in Scotland*, paper presented at Euro-Conference CELTE, University of Warwick, April 1997

KETV (Kent Education Television) (1992) *'Pilote' Primary French Course*

Kuhn, T (1962) *The Structure of Scientific Revolutions*, University of Chicago Press, London

Kyriacou, C (1991) *Effective Teaching in Schools: Theory and practice*, 2nd edition, Stanley Thorne, Cheltenham

Lapkin, S, Hart, D, and Swain, M (1991) Early and middle French immersion programs: French language outcomes, *Canadian Modern Language Review*, **48** (1), pp 11–40

Lejeune, G (1978) *Culture in Europe*, Commission of the European Community

Low, L (1999) Policy issues for primary modern languages', in *The Teaching of Modern Foreign Languages in the Primary School*, eds P Driscoll and D Frost, Routledge, London

Low, L *et al* (1993) *Evaluating Foreign Languages in Primary Schools*, Scottish CILT, Stirling

Low, L, Brown, S, Johnstone, R and Pirrie, A (1995) *Foreign Languages in Primary Schools: Evaluation of the Scottish Pilot Projects 1993–1995, Final Report*, CILT, Stirling

Martin, C (2000) Unpublished report to QCA on national and international research on the provision of modern foreign languages in the primary school

McLagan (1996) *The Times Educational Supplement/CILT Modern Language Survey of Maintained and Independent Schools in England and Wales, Scotland and Northern Ireland*, CILT, London

Mitchell, R, Martin, C and Grenfell, M (1992) *Evaluation of The Basingstoke Primary Schools Language Awareness Project: 1990–91*, Southampton University Centre for Language in Education

National Curriculum Council (1990) *Interim Report of the Modern Foreign Language Working Group*

Oller, J and Nagato, N (1974) The long term of FLES: an experiment, *Modern Language Journal*, **58**, pp 15–19

Paxman, J (1999) *The English*, Penguin, London

Pollard, A and Tann, S (1997) *Reflective Teaching in the Primary School*, Cassell, London

Radnai, Z (1996) English in primary schools in Hungary, in *Researching Languages at Primary School, Some European Perspectives*, eds P Edelenbos and R Johnstone, CILT, London

Rumley, G and Sharpe, K (2000) *Pilote Plus: Making foreign languages fun!* Kent County Council, Maidstone

SCAA (1997) *Modern Foreign Languages in the Primary Curriculum*, SCAA, London

Sharpe, K (1991) Primary French: more phoenix than dodo now, *Education 3–13*, **19** (1) pp 49–53

Sharpe, K (1992) Communication, culture, context, confidence: The four 'c's of primary modern language teaching, *Language Learning Journal*, **6**, pp 13–15

Sharpe, K (1995) The primacy of pedagogy in the early teaching of modern languages, *Language Learning Journal*, **12**, pp 40–43

Sharpe, K (1997) Mr Gradgrind and Miss Beale: Old dichotomies, inorexable choices and what shall we tell the students about primary teaching methods?, *Journal of Education for Teaching*, Vol 23, No 1, pp 69–83

Sharpe, K (1999) Modern languages in the primary school: Some implications for initial teacher training in England, in *The Teaching of Modern Languages in the Primary School*, eds P Driscoll and D Frost, Routledge, London

Sharpe, K (2000) Evaluation of the Good Practice Project: Stage one, unpublished report to CILT

Sharpe, K and Driscoll, P (2000) At what age should foreign language learning begin?, in *Issues in Modern Foreign Languages*, ed C Field, Routledge, London

Sharpe, K and Rumley, G (1993) Generalisable game activities in modern language learning, Language Learning Journal, Vol 8, pp 35–39

Shennan, Margaret (1993) *Teaching About Europe*, Cassell, London

Shorrocks, D (1993) *Implementing National Curriculum Assessment in the Primary School*, Hodder, London

Singleton, D (1989) *Language Acquisition and the Age Factor*, Multilingual Matters Ltd, Clevedon, Avon

Skender, I (1995) Elements culturels dans l'apprentissage/l'enseignement des langues entrangeres, in *Children and Foreign Languages*, ed M Vilke, University of Zagreb, Croatia

Swarbrick, A (1998) *Teaching Modern Languages*, Routledge/Open University Press, London

TGAT (1988) *National Curriclum: TGAT report: A digest*, DES, London

Trafford (1994) *Primary Foreign Languages – A fresh impetus, Proceedings of Joint ALL/NAHT Conference held in November 1992*, Association for Language Learning

Sutton, R (1991) Assessment: A framework for teachers, NFER Nelson, Windsor, p 48

Vilke, M (1988) Some psychological aspects of early second-language acquisition, *Journal of Multilingual and Multicultural Development*, **9** (1 and 2) pp 115–28

Wray, D and Medwell, J (1991) *Literacy and Language in the Primary Years*, Routledge, London, p 195

Index